Jossey-Bass Teacher

Jossey-Bass Teacher provides K–12 teachers with essential knowledge and tools to create a positive and lifelong impact on student learning. Trusted and experienced educational mentors offer practical classroom-tested and theory-based teaching resources for improving teaching practice in a broad range of grade levels and subject areas. From one educator to another, we want to be your first source to make every day your best day in teaching. *Jossey-Bass Teacher* resources serve two types of informational needs—essential knowledge and essential tools.

Essential knowledge resources provide the foundation, strategies, and methods from which teachers may design curriculum and instruction to challenge and excite their students. Connecting theory to practice, essential knowledge books rely on a solid research base and time-tested methods, offering the best ideas and guidance from many of the most experienced and well-respected experts in the field.

Essential tools save teachers time and effort by offering proven, ready-to-use materials for in-class use. Our publications include activities, assessments, exercises, instruments, games, ready reference, and more. They enhance an entire course of study, a weekly lesson, or a daily plan. These essential tools provide insightful, practical, and comprehensive materials on topics that matter most to K–12 teachers.

Teaching Tips From Your One-Minute Mentor

Quick and Easy Strategies for Classroom Success

Arnie Bianco

JOSSEY-BASS
A Wiley Imprint
www.josseybass.com

Artwork modified from illustrations originally created by Jeffrey Short.

Published by Jossey-Bass

A Wiley Imprint

989 Market Street, San Francisco, CA 94103-1741   www.josseybass.com

Jossey-Bass books and products are available through most bookstores. To contact Jossey-Bass directly call our Customer Care Department within the U.S. at 800-956-7739, outside the U.S. at 317-572-3986, or fax 317-572-4002.

Jossey-Bass also publishes its books in a variety of electronic formats. Some content that appears in print may not be available in electronic books.

Library of Congress Cataloging-in-Publication Data
Bianco, Arnie.
 Teaching tips from your one-minute mentor : quick and easy strategies for classroom success / by Arnie Bianco.
     p. cm.
 "A Wiley Imprint."
 Includes bibliographical references.
 ISBN-13: 978-0-7879-8241-6 (alk. paper)
 ISBN-10: 0-7879-8241-5 (alk. paper)
 1. Effective teaching—Handbooks, manuals, etc. I. Title.
 LB1025.3.B53 2006
 371.102—dc22
                              2006002421

Printed in the United States of America

PB Printing   10 9 8 7 6 5 4 3 2 1
FIRST EDITION

One more time:
To Deborah Ruth Bianco
for her unwavering support and encouragement
as my cheerleader extraordinaire. Thanks for being
my bookstore study buddy, personal assistant,
and coffee provider.

Contents

Introduction

A school should be the most beautiful place in every town and village . . . so beautiful that the punishment for undutiful children should be that they should be debarred from going to school the following day.

—Oscar Wilde (quoted in Maggio, 1997)

I AM AN AMERICAN EDUCATOR. My colleagues and I can be found teaching throughout the land in villages, gold coast suburbia, and our largest cities, in private schools, public schools, charter schools, church schools, and on reservations. Our mission is to prepare young learners for the challenges of tomorrow—recognizing that the nature of tomorrow is changing every day.

I am most comfortable around young people; the classroom is my milieu. I am proud to teach, and I persevere in the face of the various complexities facing our nation's education system. Educators valiantly survive in the midst of fluctuating political pressures, financial crises and constraints, a wide range of parental educational philosophies, and far-reaching media—all of which have a tremendous impact on schools and on the students who attend them.

Some of my colleagues are fortunate to have modern classrooms, adequate resources, and excellent parental support, while others confront a daily struggle against inadequate classroom space and supplies, parental apathy, and deteriorating facilities. It is most difficult to teach when hampered by unreliable heating and cooling, unsanitary restrooms, lack of storage space, security concerns, unsafe and poorly planned playgrounds, and classrooms that are ill-equipped for the technology of the twenty-first century.

Far too many kids absorb disrespect from home and peers and then bring it to school. This disrespect has created tremendous pressures on too many new teachers, who often leave the profession within the first five years. In addition, many of my experienced colleagues are so frustrated that they escape into premature retirement.

Although I am concerned about these and other larger issues that weigh heavily on my profession, I understand that my calling is not to reform the system but to bring order, structure, and a culture of appreciation to my classroom. Large issues don't show up at my door each day; kids of all varieties do.

It's not in my nature to curse the darkness. In an effort to light candles—and in the hope of assisting new teachers and other educators who need to improve their classroom management skills—I have compiled a number of quick and easy strategies for classroom success. After more than forty years as a teacher, principal, and university instructor, I'd like to share with new and established teachers what I've learned. These strategies have been influenced by many sources, including recent publications, my earlier book, *One-Minute Discipline*, visits to several hundred classrooms, ideas from other teachers, and my personal experiences.

Teaching Tips from Your One-Minute Mentor: Quick and Easy Strategies for Classroom Success is designed to educate and assist teachers in managing classroom behavior and making the most of their instructional time with students. The many strategies are presented in a format easily comprehended in a minute or two, thereby facilitating acquisition of new ideas and their application in the classroom. To survive and flourish, teachers know they must understand and meet the behavioral management challenges of today and tomorrow. These new ideas are for them.

Each chapter contains at least one powerful quotation from a collection that has formed the basis of my personal philosophy of life, both in the classroom and in my private world. These quotations support many of the classroom management strategies I suggest; the individuals who spoke or wrote them have a special ability to express a lot of wisdom in a very few words. These universal principles form a firm foundation for successful living and teaching.

I toast your caring, competence, and commitment to our most valuable resource: America's young people. With this book, I hope that, in some way, I've assisted you in this most noble endeavor.

Happy teaching.

Arnie Bianco

I AM A MASTER PAINTER, and the classroom is my canvas. I fill the canvas with faith in today, hope for tomorrow, and a love of teaching and learning. My classroom reflects this joy about learning, and it has the unmistakable hum of academic advancement, as well as the social and emotional growth of the young people who come here to learn.

I see my classroom as an assemblage of different-shaped chunks of purposeful activity. It is a center for creative thinking and achievement, where every day is a wonderful day for living and learning.

I understand that as a teacher, I wear many different hats. To fulfill this wide range of tasks, I need a great many skills and strategies. I am always adding to my toolbox and expanding my abilities.

Good teaching is built on good habits, and I do my best to develop these and to outgrow the bad habits that get in my way. Like any professional, I have a well-thought-out mission, which I refine as I grow. I learn from my mistakes and carry on.

In this chapter, I describe some fundamentals of the teaching profession.

What Is a Teacher?

Merriam Webster's Collegiate Dictionary defines *teacher* as "one whose job is to instruct." This definition, it seems to me, is incomplete because it leaves out half of the equation. A *teacher* is one whose job is to instruct *students*. This relationship—between teacher and student, expert and apprentice—should be at the heart of any definition. Over the years, that relationship has changed. Not so many years ago, it went something like this:

I am the Authority.

I will hold you Accountable.

Then I will Affirm you.

And finally Accept you.

Today, that model is quite different.

I Accept you no matter what.

I Affirm my commitment to you.

I will be Accountable for your progress.

And you will then view me as an Authority.

As a teacher, you will teach subject matter, but so much more. As many have said in different ways, you will also teach *who you are.*

> *Children have never been good at listening to their elders, but*
> *they have never failed to imitate them.*
>
> —James Baldwin (quoted in Reader's
> Digest Association, 1997)

Parker Palmer, a master teacher who has written widely on education, provides a description of a teacher that is much richer than the dictionary's bare-bones definition.

I am a teacher at heart, and there are moments in the classroom
when I can hardly hold the joy. When my students and I discov-
er unchartered territory to explore, when the pathway out of
a thicket opens before us, when our experience is illuminated
by lightning life of the mind—then teaching is the finest work
I know.

—Parker Palmer (1997)

Roles of a Teacher

We can also describe what a teacher *is* by what a teacher *does*. To be a teacher, you must be a master of not just one trade, but many. Here's an alphabetical listing of just a few of these skills.

Counselor	listens to learners
Expert resource person	develops and shares information
Facilitator	guides learning
Laboratory supervisor	provides hands-on instruction
Lecturer	conveys information
Media expert	leads discussion
Meeting leader	directs activities
Programmer	offers computer-assisted instruction
Tutor	gives one-on-one instruction

Besides needing to master these many trades, a teacher needs to know which skills are required at a given moment and be able to reach for the right tool without a minute's hesitation. As influential American educator Madeline Cheek Hunter once said,

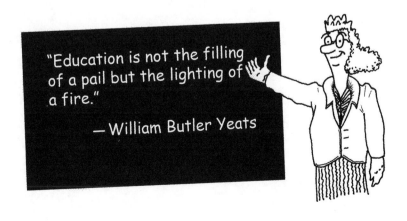

"Education is not the filling of a pail but the lighting of a fire."

—William Butler Yeats

*Teachers must be very skilled, very knowledgeable, and exquisite-
ly well-trained because neither the teacher nor the surgeon can
say, Everybody sit still until I figure out what in the heck we're
going to do next.*

                    —Madeline Cheek Hunter (quoted in Goldberg, 1990)

Great teachers are competent in all of these areas:

Knowledge of content

Knowledge of child growth and development

Familiarity with materials and how to use them

Classroom management skills

Human relations skills

Planning skills

Because what teachers do is directly
connected to their relationships with
students and others, some personal
qualities are also useful—and they're
frequently noted in the best teachers
you meet:

Teachers . . .   demonstrate a zest for
                  living and a tendency
                  to enjoy dealing with all kinds of people

                  are unconditional, vigorous advocates of young learners

                  have well-thought-out commitments and stick to them

                  run their classroom with a humble spirit and a grateful
                  humility

If the three Rs of learning are reading, writing, and 'rithmetic, then the
three Cs of teaching are caring, commitment, and competence.

I *care* about you and your academic growth.

I've been doing this for some time, and I know that I'm competent in what I know and where we're headed.

I'm *committed* to guide my students' academic, social, and emotional development. I want to make this classroom experience an important part of a great school experience.

How can you judge a teacher's professional abilities? Let's imagine that teachers are master artists, and their medium is crayons. Your mastery of teaching, then, can be expressed in the number of crayons in your crayon box.

How many crayons are in your crayon box?

- Chalk-and-talk teaching (lecture only)
- Passive students
- Very little visual reinforcement (even though 80 percent of kids are visual learners)
- Diminished interest in grade level or subject matter
- Low level of enthusiasm
- New year—same old stuff

16?

- Engages in chalk-and-talk teaching with small and large group activities
- Uses more visual reinforcement
- Has increased comfort with planning
- Feels really good about grade level and subject content
- Begins to seek out ways to stay fresh and current
- Visits other classrooms

64!!! (with the sharpener in the back)

- Has created a visual collection of pictures and materials
- Uses a variety of instructional approaches: small and large group, one-on-one, team teaching, and self-paced instruction
- Is in charge—the rabbit in its very own briar patch
- Attends workshops, conferences, and classes
- Shares ideas with and mentors other teachers
- Holds students accountable; students are actively involved and on-task

Of course, no one starts out as a master teacher. In fact, there's a rather well-traveled ladder that goes from the beginner to the master. Here's how it looks.

Novice Teacher

- Is simply trying to survive
- Has many ups and downs
- Is textbook bound
- Is very busy and "alone" at times
- Learns an enormous amount
- Finds that planning is important and time consuming
- Faces discipline and parent challenges

Advanced Beginner

- Has gained episodic knowledge (experience), which makes decisions easier
- Acquires increased grouping knowledge
- Sees similarities and connections
- Is more strategic at getting things done
- Has greater understanding of how a lesson or unit fits into the total picture

Competent Teacher
- Feels much stronger
- Discriminates curriculum decisions
- Finds that routines become automatic
- Takes responsibility
- Realizes the classroom as his or her milieu

Master Teacher
- Has a sense of the situation—knows what's going on
- Makes decisions based on lots of experience
- Uses higher-level thinking skills
- Has excellent assessment skills
- Manages class with ease and fluidity—classroom runs like a Swiss watch
- Engages in teaching that fits the vision

Creating a Mission Statement

Before you ever enter a classroom, you should have a mission statement: a set of goals that you are working toward as a teacher. As you consider what you want to say, you might want to examine some other mission statements, particularly those of teachers you admire.

The Walt Disney Company expresses its mission in just four words:

Dream   Dare   Believe   Do

The Squirrel Run School needs six:

We care . . .
We share . . .
We dare.

Here are some ideas you might consider as you build your own mission statement:

- Academic progress of every student
- Social and emotional growth of each child
- Development and creation of life skills
- Happy kids who can't wait to get to school
- Overjoyed parents who are enthusiastic supporters of their teacher and their school
- A community delighted with its educational investment
- A smile at the end of a great year

My mission statement includes these goals:

- To empower
- To impart knowledge
- To accept and respect each child unconditionally
- To provide a safe, warm, loving learning environment
- To impart skills that facilitate learning

- To open the eyes of young students to the world of learning

Once you have a mission statement, don't keep it to yourself.

Post your mission statement in the classroom so everyone can see that you eat, breathe, and sleep its principles.

Include the statement in parent newsletters.

Refer to the mission statement at your annual "Meet the Teacher" session.

Plan and schedule school activities to support your mission.

Building Habits, Making Mistakes

Old habits can't be thrown out of the upstairs window, they have to be coaxed down the stairs one step at a time.
—Mark Twain (quoted in Readers Digest Association, 1997)

We all have habits—some good, some bad. The trick is to beef up the good habits and get rid of the bad ones.

Some habits are particularly important to guard against.

Don't be a purveyor of gossip—and don't listen. Discourage others from gossiping whenever you can.

Don't find fault with people around you. This is an insidious habit. If it spreads to others, it can poison the school environment.

Don't get a swelled head. People naturally praise an excellent teacher, but if you take that praise too seriously, you can become self-centered, thus putting the interests of your reputation ahead of your students.

We all make mistakes. The goal is to decrease the number of mistakes in your overall experience.

As your experience grows, you feel worse about mistakes—you feel that you ought to know better. The thing is, just when you think you've got your diploma in experience, someone will come up with a new course requirement. You could be a teacher for a hundred years and still be greeted by a child or class that's a fresh challenge.

Experience does make us stronger, however. The trials and tribulations of your first encounter with a problem strengthen your resolve to withstand each new occurrence.

Here are a few ways to guard against mistakes:

Do your homework. Gather pertinent data before you make a big decision.

Consult with experts, supervisors or mentors, and professional friends to give you support and feedback.

Attend conferences, workshops, seminars, and graduate classes—you never know everything you need to know.

And never try to cover up a mistake—you'll only make it worse. Admit your error and promise not to repeat it. As the Chinese proverb says,

When you bow, bow low.

Your Journey to Master Teacher

As I said a few pages back, no one starts out being a master teacher. Experience is the road you take to get there, and everything you do is experience. What you experience becomes the fabric of your life as a teacher. It molds and directs your future classroom adventures. Some might call experiences *good* or *bad*, but the classification *different* is probably more accurate.

Throughout your journey as a teacher, maintain a commitment to excellence.

Never settle for mediocrity—in your efforts or in your students' efforts.

Do the right thing the right way for the right reason.

Treat all students, regardless of their background or talent, as equal in dignity and worth.

Model your dedication with vigor and enthusiasm.

As you move along the path from novice to advanced beginner to competent teacher to master, keep your eye on the goal: to be an effective and respected teacher.

If you **WANT** to be different, **YOU** have to **DO** different.

Here's what you'll look like:

- You have a positive attitude when dealing with all kinds of kids and parents—and the opportunities they present.

- You optimize any and all situations, even the ugly ones, by using your damage-control skills.

- You keep your commitments—you're always where you're supposed to be when you're supposed to be there.

- You keep alive the "big ideas" that led you to a teaching career, continuing to nurture not just your professional development but your hopes and dreams, as well.

Only the Brave Should Teach

Only the brave,
Only the brave should teach.
Only those who love the young should teach.
Teaching is a vocation.
It is as sacred as the priesthood;
as innate a desire, as inescapable
as the genius which compels an artist.
If one has not the concern for humanity,
the love of living creatures,
the vision of the priest and the artist,
one must not teach.

                —Pearl S. Buck (quoted in Lipscomb, Webb, and Conn, 1994)

Chapter 2

Getting to Know Your Students

MY STUDENTS ARE the school's clients. It's important for me to understand them as individuals and to form a good relationship with each and every one. I begin with knowledge about the intellectual and emotional development of youngsters at their age. Then I get to know each child's background and interests, skills and needs. I meet with each student on a regular basis, and I keep individual records of their progress.

It's my responsibility to lead all my students to achievements in academics and in the life skills they will need in the years ahead. Respect and responsibility, along with consideration for others, are an important part of my curriculum. I model these character traits for them. I use tact in my conversations with them, and I never talk down to them.

As I develop relationships with each of my students, I do my best to let all of them know how much I value them and how committed I am to their progress. Knowing that their teacher cares about them makes an enormous contribution to students' learning.

In this chapter, I offer some suggestions for getting to know your students and developing a strong and positive bond.

Bloom's Taxonomy: Cognitive Skills

There are a number of ways to understand cognitive skills and how students learn. One of the most widely used was developed by a fellow named Benjamin Bloom and a group of educational psychologists.

Their "taxonomy" includes six basic learning skills in a hierarchy, from the bottom up: Knowledge, Comprehension, Application, Analysis, Synthesis, and Evaluation.

The descriptions provided here will help you understand what skills Bloom is describing. The verbs are particularly helpful in identifying the level of your students' skills—and the level that your test questions might be assessing.

Knowledge

Student recalls or recognizes information, ideas, and principles in the appropriate form in which they are learned.

Terms

Define	List
Recite	Name
Locate	Match
Identify	Memorize
Recall	

Comprehension

Student translates, comprehends, or interprets information based on prior learning.

Terms

Explain	Illustrate
Paraphrase	Estimate
Convert	Translate
Interpret	Infer
Rewrite	

Application

Student selects, transfers, and uses data and principles to complete a life problem task with a minimum of direction.

Terms

Apply	Operate
Solve	Compute
Show	Experiment

Analysis

Student is aware of thought process in use and can examine, classify, hypothesize, collect data, and draw conclusions to the nature or structure of a question.

Terms

Examine	Categorize
Graph	Chart
Organize	Outline
Discriminate	Diagram
Compare and contrast	

Synthesis

Student originates, integrates, and combines ideas into a product, plan, or proposal that is new.

Terms

Combine	Rearrange
Create	Develop
Pretend	Design
Invent	Improve
Compose	

Evaluation

Student appraises, assesses, or criticizes on a basis of specific standards and criteria (this does not include opinion unless standards are made explicit).

Terms

Judge	Select
Support	Prioritize
Justify	Criticize
Debate	Recommend

Understanding Emotional Development

Kids also develop emotionally as they get older. A great deal of research talks about what kinds of emotional issues are related to different age groups, and you can easily locate your age group in any library. Here, for example, are some traits associated with kids in middle or junior high school.

Sometimes, there's no talking to those hormones... they're so emotional.

Emotional Changes

- Shyness and noisiness
- Exaggerated responses to anything with sexual implications
- Desire for any kind of attention
- Ignorance, ridicule of adult convention

Intellectual Characteristics

- Pressure to succeed academically
- Heightened egocentrism
- Wide range of skills, interests, and abilities
- Increased concern with moral and ethical issues

Physical Changes

- Weight and height gain
- Sexual maturation
- Periods of hyperactivity and fatigue
- Poorly selected foods

Social Changes

- Feels diminished allegiance to parents
- Needs social acceptance of peers
- Demands independence
- Works for rewards

Your students will have a variety of emotional needs, too, and you'll need to keep these in mind to ensure maximum learning and a positive classroom environment.

To understand where each of your students stands cognitively and emotionally, you need to get to know them. I've found a couple of ways to gather a lot of information about everyone very quickly as the school year begins.

Backpack Introductions

On the first day of school, bring a backpack to class with objects related to your life experience—old report cards, pictures of family and pets, travel souvenirs, awards, hobby paraphernalia—and use them to tell the students about yourself.

Then set aside time each day so that all of the students can bring their own backpack of treasures to show the class. You get to know your students, they get to know each other, and each student gets a moment in the spotlight.

Student Shields

Another idea is to ask students to draw a personal "coat of arms," depicting the things that are most important to them. These shields can be displayed on bulletin boards for a while and eventually find a home in your student information folder.

Creating and maintaining individual student folders lets you keep a variety of information about each kid—anecdotal notes, completed papers, home contacts, and family information—in a place where it's easy to track down. Besides organizing information about your students, the individual student folders will give your kids absolute proof that you see each of them as an individual you want to know better. The folders are also great to use during parent conferences.

Individual Pupil's Folders Should Include . . .

- Parent contacts (copies of notes and a record of calls to parents)

- A representative sampling of the year's class work

- Teacher-made tests

- Pertinent anecdotal or discipline reports

- Individual action plan records

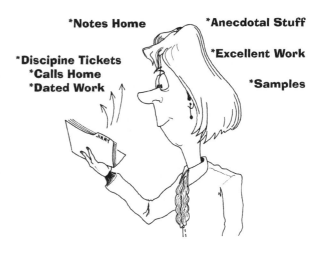

*Notes Home
*Anecdotal Stuff
*Excellent Work
*Discipine Tickets
*Calls Home
*Dated Work
*Samples

More Information-Gathering Strategies

As the school year continues, you'll find other techniques for gathering information about your students. You might ask them to complete a reinforcer survey. The sample here is general, but you could tailor surveys to particular issues.

Reinforcer Survey

After school I like to _____

My favorite TV program is _____

My favorite activity at school is _____

My best friend is _____

My favorite CD is _____

My favorite subject is _____

I like to read books about _____

My hobby is _____

My favorite pet is _____

Three things I like to do most are _____

You could also ask your students to write in a journal every day. Let them know that you'll be reading their entries so that they can tell you what's on their mind and even ask for a chat if they want to talk with you.

Assure them that what they write in the journal will be strictly between the two of you—and, of course, you'll keep your promise.

Asking parents to provide information about their children gives you inside information about each kid. It also tells the parents not only that you're interested in their child but also that you view them as partners in the education of their son or daughter.

Please Tell Me about Your Child

We are off to a great start this year. I have established an individual progress folder on each student in our class. I would like to add a short information page from you. I will be sharing academic and social progress with you at our first conference and throughout the year.

Please include such things as your child's:

history	likes and dislikes	sports
friends	favorite food	hobbies
vacations	books	dreams
habits	fun activities	TV shows

Dear teacher:

_____

_____

_____

_____

_____

_____

_____

_____

_____

_____

Building Good Relationships

Of course, the goal of all this effort isn't simply data collection. The information gathering will let your students now you're interested them, and it will also give you ways to connect with them—asking about their hobbies or pets or other interests.

When your students know they matter, you've made a great start toward everything else that will happen in your classroom. Building on this foundation, you can go forward to build solid relationships with your students. You like kids—that's part of the reason you're a teacher. So connecting with them is just in your nature.

There's a simple formula for building a successful relationship:

Good times – bad times = our relationship

You'll want to do your best to reduce the bad times and create as many good times as possible. Another way to look at this is that you're establishing a positive feeling tone. Base your classroom philosophy on support, acceptance, and "controlled chaos." Create a classroom that is warmed by *congenial fires.*

When your relationship works, students will see you as a real person not just as The Teacher. To create this bond you need to listen to them with empathy, paying close attention to what they say and trying to connect with the underlying emotions. In the process, you also begin to teach them life skills.

Realness Means . . .

You are a genuine person.

You express enthusiasm.

You understand kids' feelings.

Empathic Listening Means . . .

You are sensitive to kids' feelings.

Students feel they can relate to you.

Teaching Life Skills

Respect: Value the worth of another person.

Initiative: Do something because it needs to be done.

Responsibility: Do what you're supposed to do when you're supposed to do it.

Friendship: Make a friend so that you care for and trust each other.

Problem solving: Solve problems, even when it is very difficult.

Organization: Plan ahead to keep things in order.

Common sense: Use good judgment.

Cooperation: Work together toward a common goal or purpose.

Curiosity: Want to know more about one's world.

Patience: Wait calmly for someone or something.

Courage: Act according to one's belief.

Caring: Be concerned for others.

Integrity: Do the right thing.

Effort: Try your hardest.

Perseverance: Keep trying no matter what.

Making Contact

I believe the greatest gift I can conceive of having from anyone is to be seen by them, heard by them. The greatest gift I can give is to see, hear, understand, and to touch another person.

When this is done I feel contact has been made.

—Virginia Satir

Making contact with your students is the foundation for everything that will happen in your classroom.

Chapter 3

Creating a Culture of Appreciation

AFTER YEARS OF TEACHING, I understand that I create the climate in my classroom. I have a powerful influence over the kids who come here day after day to learn. My demeanor and my attitude can make their day stormy or sunny, can make them morose or joyful. I can use my teaching tools to torture or inspire, to humiliate or humor, hurt or heal, discourage or support.

I choose the positive. I work hard at *connecting* and minimize my *correcting*. I have developed management skills that praise and reinforce the efforts and contributions of my kids. As a result, almost all classroom time is devoted to instruction.

I show my gratitude for the privilege of teaching young Americans by making student appreciation a way of life. My teacher energy is directed at providing a warm, accepting, safe, and structured classroom environment: a culture of appreciation.

In this chapter, I'll offer some suggestions for creating a similar climate in your classroom.

Build a Good Basic Structure

As a teacher, you are a social architect. You are responsible for creating a learning environment, a "structure," that is safe, caring, and academically successful.

Here are some of the basic building materials you can use to build a culture of appreciation:

- Kind words of support and respect

- Visual signs of approval—a thumbs-up, a big smile, a hug, a high-five, eye contact with a smile

- Public and private written kudos

- Expressions of confidence when a kid proposes a new idea or project: "You are a hard worker and have a great track record—I know that you can do it again."

- Expanded learning experiences as earned privileges—guest speakers, dances, field trips—ask your class what they would like as a payoff

Create a Culture of Appreciation

Lead a Cheer

Borrow some strategies from the world of team sports. Get each day off to a good start by leading a cheer.

Teacher	Kids
Why are we here?	To learn.
What will we give today?	Our very best!
What will we get from today?	Everything we can.
What matters?	Learning matters.
What else matters?	We matter!
How smart are we?	Very smart.
How creative are we?	Very creative.
Where are we headed?	To a successful tomorrow.
Where else are we headed?	To college!

Be a Classroom Coach

Let the kids select a team mascot and give him a place of honor in your classroom.

Celebrate individual or group achievement by asking the kids to join you in a silent cheer. Class members repeatedly raise their hands in a *totally quiet* pumping motion. You could also let the honored student do an end zone dance or a (controlled) lap around the classroom, receiving high fives and accolades from classmates.

Make a Wall of Fame where you post the names and pictures of students who have been honored for academic achievement, sports, and school or community service.

Rewarding students for their achievements—or good behavior—is a great motivator, and at the same time, it builds that positive feeling tone you want in your classroom. A couple of simple techniques provide rewards.

"Let's have a silent cheer for Arnoldo!"

A Raffle for Rewards

Get a roll of tickets and begin a campaign of rewarding good behavior and academic progress.

When a young learner gets a ticket, she puts her name on the back of the ticket and places it in the raffle jar.

The teacher sets the time requirement (one week, a month, and so forth) for the raffle drawing.

Kids know that the more tickets they get the better their chances.

You can also establish a Token Economy in your classroom, using fake currency (maybe with you playing George Washington) or marbles, chips, stars—anything you can give students to motivate behavior you're encouraging. Your picture goes on the front:. . .

And a list of behaviors you're rewarding goes on the back:

_____ has earned a bonus buck for

___ Honesty ___ Knowledge ___ Respect for others

___ Integrity ___ Helpfulness ___ Politeness

___ Citizenship ___ Caring attitude ___ Academic excellence

___ Special service ___ Freedom of thought and action ___ Consideration of others

___ Other _____

_____ Teacher signature

Here's how it works:

Give out dollars as a reward to individuals or groups.

Students can exchange these for popcorn parties, movie tickets, computer time, trinkets, chitchat time—any creative payoff that you and your class can devise.

You'll have to decide when and how often you'll let students redeem their dollars or other tokens for rewards. It's a good idea to make the time span relatively short so student enthusiasm stays high.

Payoffs for Positive Results

For something with a quicker payoff, create a Star of the Day program. Establish some criteria, and let your students know what they are. Then designate a set of privileges that only the star of the day can enjoy. Here are some ideas:

- Special messenger duty
- A seat of honor—maybe an easy chair you brought from home
- Lunch in the classroom
- First place in line for recess or lunch or dismissal

And you might want to take suggestions from the class.

I am "STAR of the day!" My exclusive privileges include: a special seat, first in line, a free homework pass, and a big, warm smile from my teacher!

The Whole Class Wins

Or instead of rewarding one special person, you can take one special day to reward *all* students. How about

Fabulous Friday!
Fantastic Friday!
Freedom Friday!

Take one class period or part of the day to provide an academic payoff rewarding student effort and hard work. Anything that breaks from the routine can provide a reward—games, free reading, a relevant video, or time to get a head start on weekend homework. Or you could match the reward to the effort you've observed.

To qualify, kids must

- Complete a certain number of required assignments

- Earn a required number of points during the week

Small Decencies and Warm Fuzzies

So far I've shown you a number of tangible ways to reward positive achievement and behavior and establish a culture of appreciation, but there are a million small ways to let your kids know they're special.

You could start with Small Decencies (a kind word, a smile, a friendly pat on the back, or a high five)—*I must make sure that each child knows how much I care about him or her . . .*

I don't care how much you know, until I know how much you care.

. . . and Warm Fuzzies (praise tied to acceptable behavior and delivered on the spot).

Make your kids feel how much you appreciate their skills and behavior—and just the opportunity to spend time being with them.

Words of Affirmation

- Honest delight in student efforts and achievements
- Genuine (earned) compliments
- "I'm with you!" "What a great class (thinker, citizen)!"

Gifts

- Sticky praise note on desk
- Reward certificates or token economies
- Free time

Quality Time

- One-on-one personal interview
- Counseling assistance
- College recommendations or sharing of experiences
- Home calls or visits
- Attendance of a student's athletic event or performance

Physical Touch

- High-fives

- A hug or a handshake as (young) kids leave classroom

Remember to stay positive . . .

Always include a strength-based assessment in any student report; list personal strong points, interests, learning style, and academic strengths.

Place the letter P under your clock as a reminder to stay positive.

Keep ten pennies in your pocket and lay one on your desk throughout the day whenever you praise individuals or the class. Aim to empty your pocket more than once.

"I love to cooperate when my teacher is so positive."

. . . and say no to negativity.

A negative statement may get quick results, but it has to be repeated again and again. It seldom accomplishes long-term results.

The bottom third of an average class gets ten times more corrective feedback. Make a concerted effort to spread your attention around the entire classroom

Evaluate Yourself

To make sure you're on target—being positive instead of negative—you might see whether you can find someone to help assess your performance, using this interaction tally sheet.

		September 14-28	
	Students	Positive	Negative
~~	Debbie	IIIII	II
~~	Julie	III	IIIII II
~~	Caitlin	IIIII I	I
~~	Peter	II	III
~~	Joe	IIIII III	IIIII
~~	Arnoldo	IIII	IIIII II
~~	Virginia	III	IIIII

Designate a tally person (aide or responsible student) and *train* them in what constitutes a positive or negative interaction between the teacher and the total class.

Ask them to observe you in class and compile data.

After a set period of time (usually a month), you will have important data on which kids are being called on and the nature of teacher-student interactions.

Make specific goals based on the data and then "test" (repeat) again in about six weeks.

Go an Extra Mile

Building a culture of appreciation, however, is a hard thing to measure. You'll know it when you see it, and so will your students. Go the extra mile for your kids—that extra mile is never crowded. Here are some thoughts to keep in mind on that journey.

*People judge you for your actions, not your intentions. You may
have a heart of gold, but so has a hard-boiled egg.*
—Good Reading (quoted in Reader's Digest Association, 1997)

*Appreciation is like an insurance policy. It has to be renewed
every now and then.*
—Dave McIntyre (quoted in Reader's Digest Association, 1997)

Silent gratitude isn't very much use to anyone.
—G. B. Stern (quoted in Reader's Digest Association, 1997)

*I now perceive one immense omission in my psychology—
the deepest principle of Human Nature is the craving to be
appreciated.*
—William James (quoted in Reader's Digest Association, 1997)

It's too late for William James to put his wisdom into practice, but *you*
can start today to show each child in your class how much he or she matters to you.

MY CLASSROOM IS my milieu—I have a very high comfort level around young learners. My kids are an endless source of fun and amazement, and the learning moments when they "get it" are more than worth my effort.

My goal is to turn all of my students into active learners, fully engaged in mastering their subjects. I speak about 150 words per minute, while my students listen at 400 words per minute. I need to make sure that their brains are tuned in and on task.

To do this, I give my students the relevant background, and then I encourage them to go forward on their own. The traditional hands up–hands down (teacher asks question–student responds) approach is just one way of checking for pupil understanding. I use other techniques, as well, to make them think creatively and take risks.

As a teacher, I am not a soloist, performing at the front of the classroom. I am the conductor of an orchestra composed of my students—each and every one contributes to our performance.

In this chapter, I share some of my time-tested techniques for turning out a class full of enthusiastic, energetic learners, ready for the next challenge.

Creating Active Learners

To move your students into the orchestra—to make sure they're participating in the symphony of learning you conduct—you may need to change your style of questions and answers, with an emphasis on the former.

Teacher as Soloist: Less Active Learners	Teacher as Conductor: More Active Learners
"With this card and these blocks we are going to …"	"I'm going to show you a card and some blocks. What do you think we are going to do?"
Call on a student and ask a question.	Ask a question. Wait. Call on a student.
Student gives an answer, and teacher repeats it.	Student gives an answer, and the teacher calls on another student to repeat the answer.
Student asks: "Now what do we do?"	Answer the question with a question.
"With these sentence strips, I want you to …"	"Knowing what you now know, what do you think we will do with these sentence strips?"
"On page 12, I want you to …"	"At the top of page 12 is a box. Who is brave enough to tell me what we are going to do?"

Here are a few ways to get students to participate in class. Once you've introduced these ideas to students, you can use them again and again throughout the school year with the simplest signal to introduce them.

Traditional Hand Raising. Boring when used all the time, but still a good tool.

Sweat Box. Kids put their names on wooden sticks or slips of paper, and the teacher draws names randomly out of the box. All students listen and are on task.

Choral Response. Create a signal that tells students you want them to repeat what you said in unison. This verbally emphasizes a point, and the class reinforces what they've learned.

Scanner. Use your index finger or a tool of some kind, and point it around the class, making a scanning noise. Then let it point at a student. Be unpredictable.

Echo. Call on a student and then have another student (or more than one student) *repeat* exactly what was said. You can vary this by having them echo the content using their own words.

Beanie Baby. Toss a Beanie Baby to the student you're calling on. After the student answers, he or she tosses it back to you or to another student. Be creative with your own variations.

Great One-liners for Active Learners

Need more strategies for encouraging students to become independent thinkers? Here are some conversational ploys for drawing student participation:

Which one would you choose?

I challenge you to . . .

Tell me how you did that.

What do you think might happen?

What do you do next?

Why is that one better?

Showing While Telling

About 80 percent of people are visual learners. They absorb information best through their eyes. That's why you want to be sure to supplement your instruction with visual aids, such as charts, videos, word pictures, and other media.

Making Their Brains Sweat

When people exercise their bodies, they work up a sweat. Your goal should be to give your students (metaphorically) sweating brains. When you ask the question before you call on a student, you make sure that all your students are thinking of an answer.

There are several benefits to that small pause between asking the question and calling on a specific student:

- Teachers ask higher-level questions.

- Students ask more questions.

- The number of appropriate responses increases.

- Failures to respond decrease.

- Contributions by "slow" students increase.

You can use these lines to encourage the students you call on:

To make this work, students have to know that it's safe to reply—they won't be scolded or humiliated by you or by other students if they give the wrong answer.

At the beginning of the year, tell your class that you have put a personal safety net under each and every one—a soft place to fall. Tell them you want them to take risks, and you'll praise and reward them for doing so.

Encouraging Risk

To make your point, set up a Risky Business Board in your classroom, honoring students with a star when they take a calculated risk. You might add the saying:

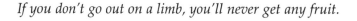

If you don't go out on a limb, you'll never get any fruit.

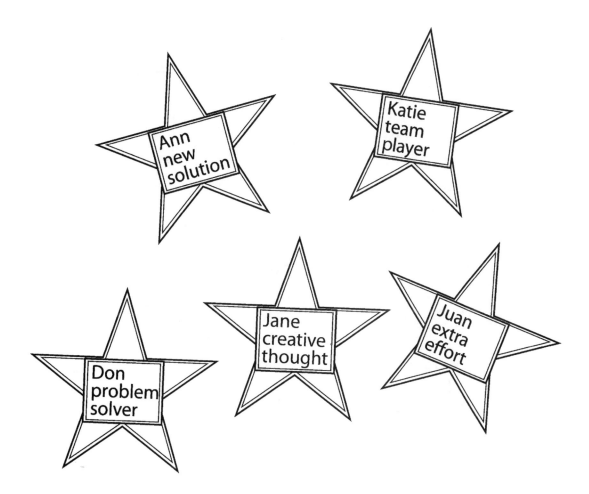

Changing Subjects

Tossing a Beanie Baby—or a bean bag or softball—to students as you call on them puts a little excitement into reviewing old subjects before the class moves on.

You might also use the Exit Strategy described here.

Have students line up at the classroom door.

Stand at the door and ask pertinent review questions.

Students who answer correctly get to go home early or return to their seats to chat with friends until the bell.

Students who answer incorrectly have to go back to the end of the line and try again.

Using the Exit Strategy, all of your students are held accountable, and good listeners are rewarded with some free time.

Retention is increased when teachers provide a bridge between old and new material. For example:

When you're introducing a whole new unit, try using the Big Brain Poster.

Tell students what the new subject is, and ask each one to write a sentence or a fact—anything they know about the new topic—on a three-by-five card or sticky note.

Then have them put the sticky notes on the Big Brain Poster.

Reviewing the cards will give you a general idea of what the students already know, so that you can move forward at their speed.

You might also consider removing and discussing each card—at random or organized in specific categories or groups.

Giving Students the Support They Need

When students are working at their desks, you can pass through the aisles to give some one-on-one support. Move from student to student, reteaching, assisting, and encouraging, as needed. To paraphrase Julius Caesar:

I praise . . . I prompt . . . I leave

Some students are bound to need more extensive help. Here are some ways to let them identify themselves, so you can keep an eye out for trouble spots and fix them as quickly as possible.

"Can you help with my vocab?"

"Can you help with my math?"

"May I go to the bathroom?"

"May I go to the office?"

"Can we go outside?"

"Can you tell Johnny to stop?"

Glue red and blue plastic cups together at the rim. Students who need help put the red cup to the top.

Have students make "Help me" signs. When they need help they put up the sign.

Students who need help put their name on the board. You take care of them in order.

Students write a detailed note telling you what they need. When you have the time, you respond to each request.

Hurdle Help is an assistance plan you can use whenever you see that a student is bogged down on an assignment.

Tell the student: "Let me help you with that one. . . ."

"Now let me see you do one. . . ."

"Very good. Now do two more and bring them back for me to check."

When the student brings back two correct problems or answers, say, "Very good! Now complete the row and bring it back to me."

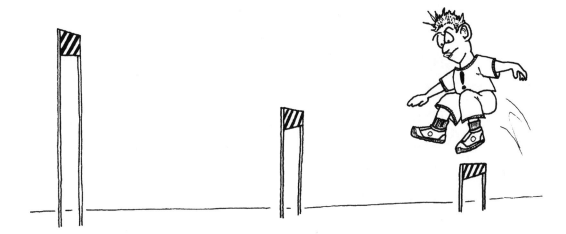

When the student returns: "Excellent! You are now ready to complete the assignment on your own."

Validate the parts of the assignment that are done correctly.

Praise for what's right and train for what's wrong.

Marking Time

Classes will often experience a "sugar low" near the end of a class period and particularly right before lunch or dismissal. You can provide verbal encouragement reminding them that the end is at hand:

> You people are doing just great! We have about eight minutes to go.

> I appreciate your hard work. We're coming up on lunch in about seven minutes.

> Five minutes to go. The end is in sight!

Another time-related strategy is to keep in your classroom a chart of rewards that early finishers on tests or assignments can enjoy.

Help a friend

Go to reading center

Do homework

Go to game center

Study for a test

Go to listening center

Have silent reading time

Complete journal writing

Study for spelling test

Complete work on your project

Playing Games

Another way to restore flagging enthusiasm is to use games to teach. Several old standards plus popular TV and board games are easily adapted to fit the subject matter. Bingo, Scrabble, and Trivial Pursuit are just some examples.

Board games can also serve as "sponge activities," ways to use valuable time when your lesson plans are completed sooner than expected. Here are some others.

- Review worksheets and parts of past texts

- Drill exercises

- Review material from previous lessons

- DOL, DOM, and DOG (Daily Oral Language, Daily Oral Math, Daily Oral Geography), commercial chart activities that can be purchased from a teaching tools store, catalog, or online resource

> *You cannot help men permanently by doing for them what they could or should do for themselves.*
> —William J. H. Boetcker

Underlying all the other goals you have as a teacher in today's schools is the most important one: to create independent thinkers for tomorrow. Challenge your students to use their own minds. Provide activities that stimulate their brains. Then celebrate their independent thinking and acting.

Chapter
5

Setting Up
Your Classroom

I UNDERSTAND that the youngsters in my care look to me to create a structure in which they can thrive. I also understand that someone has to be in charge. In my classroom, I'm always in charge, and I aim to establish an orderly, positive environment for living and learning.

I start each school year by organizing my classroom, both its physical space and behavioral guidelines. On the very first day, I set forth my standards and expectations, and then I stay as consistent as possible. Throughout the year, I revisit and review these principles to make sure everyone in my class is on the same page.

Research supports the idea that classroom management has the greatest effect on student learning—more than cognitive processes, home environment, curriculum design, and school demographics or culture. In return, I believe that good instructional practices—like the ones I described in Chapter Four—make an important contribution to classroom management. Time is a precious commodity. You want to spend yours on teaching, not on tasks related to student control.

In this chapter, I describe some measures you can take to ensure a disciplined environment in your classroom, where learning, work, fun, and praise take up most of your time, and behavior problems are kept to a minimum.

Discipline = to Instruct

You will find that you can avoid many disciplinary issues by paying attention to the strategies we've discussed in previous chapters: getting to know your students, building a culture of appreciation, and establishing a good teaching style.

One of the biggest causes of discipline problems may be anonymity. Make sure you know each of your young learners as an individual—and let each one know you care. You might want to schedule personal interviews with your students to discuss their academic progress and what's happening in their out-of-school lives.

It's interesting that the Latin root of the word *discipline* means "to instruct," not "to punish." Sometimes instructional issues can have consequences in behavioral problems. You might want to check the list for a behavioral symptom and see whether the instructional diagnosis matches the situation in your classroom.

Instructional Diagnosis	Behavioral Symptom
Assignments are too light	Students are unmotivated, make no progress
Assignments are too heavy	Students get revenge by misbehaving
Assignments are poorly planned	Classroom features off-task behavior
Work is merely verbal	Classroom features restlessness and noise
Work is poorly scheduled	Students are exhausted or fatigued
Subject matter is too easy	Students are bored, unchallenged
Subject matter is too hard	Students seem frustrated, act as though "I don't care"
Teacher talks over kids heads	Students feel out of place

Tactical Issues

The classroom environment is enhanced by the seating arrangement. Where you put the seats, chairs, or tables can have a positive impact on student behavior. You want an arrangement that lets you get close to all the students as easily as possible.

The quietest area in your classroom will always be in the area where you're standing—students see it as the high-risk zone.

To ensure a classroom that's all-over quiet, then, you want to keep the high-risk zone moving—in other words,

TWWA = Teach While Walking Around

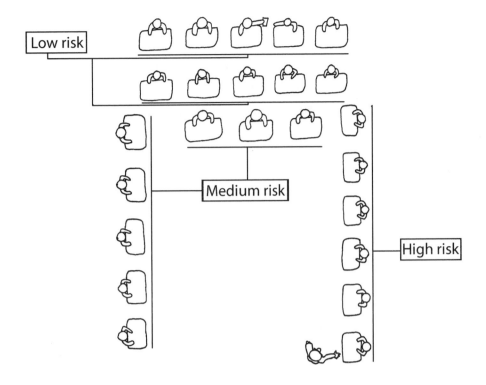

Moving around the classroom, you can stop to encourage or prompt, praise or let your presence be felt, monitor and adjust instruction. TWWA is an important instructional tool.

Take a lesson from this little poem:

The decent docent doesn't doze;
He teaches standing on his toes.
His students dassn't doze and does
And that's what teaching is and was.

Teacher With-It-ness

Moving around the classroom while you teach is just one element of "with-it-ness." The idea is that you're totally attuned to your students and your classroom—and your students know it.

Being with-it means

- You have eyes in the back of your head—you can see the whole class even though you may seem to be looking in only one direction.

- You anticipate problems and address them ASAP.

- You're always ready to abandon one lesson and move to another activity. You're ready to use peer pressure, if needed, or as a last resort, remove "the perp" from the area.

- If interest wanes, you change activities or exercise the troops—the teacher may need a break, too.

Remember that students don't have an adult attention span. A change of activity is required regularly—not necessarily a change of lesson, but a change of focus. Calculate the attention span by adding and subtracting two from the age of the students. In other words, twelve-year-olds have an attention span of ten to fourteen minutes.

Use a check-in procedure with your students to make sure they understand what is expected. Ask:

What did I ask you to do?

Did you understand what I said?

Were my directions clear?

Tell me in your own words what you heard me say.

Another aspect of teacher with-it-ness is being organized. Make sure you know exactly what your class is going to do and in what order.

9:00	Greet kids.
9:01	Pledge
9:02	Song
9:04	Attendance
9:05	Begin briefing
9:06	Continue briefing
9:07	Summarize briefing

Creating Routines

In the regular order of classroom business, you'll experience breaks when you change from one subject to another, get ready for lunch or dismissal, or switch activities. These breaks are invitations to off-task behavior and unnecessary delay.

- Develop routines that smooth out the jerkiness of these transitions.

- Explain the routines to students and let them practice.

- Use time transitions—it could be a competitive activity.

And don't forget to reward the class when they've mastered these routines.

A routine that's particularly useful is one that gets the kids ready for a new instructional period. When you give the signal, say . . .

Students are trained to follow these steps:

- Desks cleared completely except for a pencil

- Eyes on teacher

- Absolute quiet

- Brains engaged

You reward their total compliance.

An extension of this strategy is to develop one-word signals for commands you frequently give. For example:

Gum	Throw your gum away.
Please	Pick up the area around your desk.

There's no need to use a student's name with the command, but if necessary, move closer to the student and repeat the word.

Making Rules

Like routines, rules are necessary to the smooth functioning of any classroom. Setting the class's rules should be your first order of business when the school year begins. You may want to start with some basic rules of your own.

1. Bring all materials to class.
2. Be in your seat and ready when class starts.
3. Get permission before speaking.
4. Respect all people and their property.

There are a number of areas where rules might be useful.

Class Rules List

Respect	Conduct	Treatment of others
Safety	Movement	Materials
Food	Cheating	Participation
Equipment	Passes	Make-up work
Clothing	Tardiness	Private property
Talking	Visitors	Illegal substances

You may want to let students participate in some of the rule making. Doing so will make them feel empowered, and they may be more likely to follow rules they had a role in making.

Thank you for letting us work on the class rules, and I also like it when we can vote on things.

Your rule making should have these characteristics . . .

Student input

Standards

Consistency

Positive plans

Fair, firm, and friendly

Clear expectations

. . . *and* they should be made during the first week of school.
One more thing:

Any rule that makes
a little girl cry has got
to be a bad rule.

More Rule Making

Some rules fall neatly into a never–always opposition. They set boundaries for students and define the habits that will make students successful in your classroom. You can review this list with your students on the first day of school and post it somewhere in your room for the rest of the year:

Never . . .	Always . . .
Hurt anyone	Come prepared to school
Cheat	Be punctual
Bring food or gum into class	Use common courtesy
Put anyone down	Use appropriate language
	Show respect and tolerance for fellow classmates
	Follow directions

It's important to understand from the start that some of your students will test your standards and your commitment to the established rules. Never make a demand that you're not prepared to follow through on. Kids need to know that if they break an established rule or procedure, they can predict the consequence with 100 percent accuracy.

Sure, go ahead and break my face!

They should know that you will always listen to their explanation or their side of the story. But they also should understand that life can be unpredictable and unfair. Some decisions you make will not be discussed with the class. Let them know that you'll be as fair as humanly possible, but that you are nevertheless in charge—and they're not.

I will be fair, AND I won't always be equal.

Always do what you say you are going to do. It is the glue that binds successful relationships.

—Jeffrey Timmons (1989)

It is easier to resist at the beginning than at the end.
—Leonardo da Vinci (quoted in Covey, 1989).

I can't think of two better pieces of advice for teachers. Setting rules must be done at the start of the school year—not on the fly as situations arise. And students must understand that the rules are the rules. When you provide students with standards and expectable results, you're giving them a safe place to learn.

I PROVIDE MY STUDENTS with the feedback that will help them learn how to grow into thriving adults and socially adept citizens. I help them distinguish between behaviors that are appropriate and those that are not.

One basic strategy is to give students a choice between a goal (what I want them to do) and a consequence (the result of their failure to cooperate). I'm giving them the power to choose, and at the same time I'm offering a strong incentive to make the right choice.

I explain to my students that our classroom—and life—is filled with wonderful opportunities. Each opportunity requires responsible action, and responsible actions lead to more opportunities. Irresponsible actions, on the other hand, lead to a hierarchy of consequences. When I discipline, I use an age-appropriate, graduated system, consistently trying the BB gun long before I bring out the cannon.

Many kids suffer from cognitive overload and easily become "teacher deaf." I reduce the amount of teacher verbiage they have to handle by using simple visual cues and judicious verbal strategies to keep them out of trouble and in my good graces. This chapter describes several of these techniques.

Anticipating Trouble

Research suggests that more than 50 percent of classroom time is taken up with noninstructional work—in other words, keeping order takes more time than teaching kids. It's certainly true that most kids cause trouble once in a while, and some kids cause trouble quite often.

Many kids have had years to develop bad habits and behaviors. They may have discovered a number of tactics or manipulations that bring the desired result—getting what they want. Some kids become experts at a particular approach, while others are adept at using them all.

Badgering and nagging

Temper (intimidation)

Threat (anger)

Martyrdom

Physical force

Buttering up teacher

Sometimes you will get frustrated having to deal with these issues—but it's your job to seek out effective interventions. Keep on trying until you find something that works. Never give up.

Rewards and Consequences

Persuading your students to adopt appropriate behavior means providing consistent and appropriate consequences when they make the incorrect choice. It's important to give students a clear, either-or choice and then follow through. No discussion: students may try to engage you in chatter to get attention—which was probably the idea of the inappropriate behavior in the first place.

A powerful strategy is to give the transgressor an opportunity to recommend three possible consequences. Make it clear that you reserve the

The Mutual Consequence Plan

I have to come up with three possible consequences and meet with her on Monday.

right to modify the suggestions or impose your own consequence if none of the suggestions seem appropriate to you. With serious infractions, you may want to give the offender a day or two to think up potential consequences—and ponder how he or she got into this trouble in the first place.

On the other side, it's also important to reward responsible behavior with privileges—just as consistently as you impose consequences.

Consider setting up a system of reward-consequences cards. You can start with two traditional decks and paste "reward" and "consequence" language to their faces. Students who behave will get to draw a reward from the deck, while students who make the wrong choices draw their own consequences. Here are some ideas.

Rewards:

Free paperback book	Five bonus homework points	First out to lunch for one week
One point toward class pizza party (five needed)	Free snack from snack jar	Lunch with teacher and a friend
One-day homework pass	Fifteen-minute game period for the whole class	Five bonus test points

Consequences:

Last out at dismissal	See teacher after class
Last out at lunch	Call to parent

Be a Positive Critic

Some of us *tend* to be negative, even though most of us don't *intend* to be. In fact, research shows that after second grade, the reprimand and correction rate exceeds praise and reinforcement by two to one. If you put your mind to it, you don't have to do it that way.

Develop your skills for constructive criticism:

- Criticize in private.

- Don't show anger.

- Condemn the sin and not the sinner.

- Avoid the word *you.*

- Let the offender suggest a remedy.

- Insist on a real commitment to change.

- Don't "soften" the impact. You want the impression to stick.

Find some way to keep track of your praise and positive strokes, and watch for their balance against reprimands and corrections.

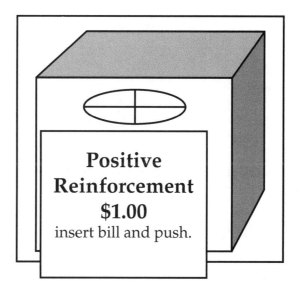

The Sandwich Technique

An interesting strategy for giving both praise and corrections—while reversing the two-to-one ratio—is called the Sandwich Technique. To use it, "sandwich" your reprimand or correction between two slices of praise and reinforcement.

Here are some examples:

This part is exactly right.

You may want to rethink that statement.

I think your general approach is very good.

The first row is correct.

Number 12 needs work.

The rest looks really great.

I know I can always rely on you to be helpful.

I'd appreciate more help in this area.

I'm very proud of your effort.

Using Body Language

When you're hoping to deliver a message to your students, keep in mind this breakdown of how kids receive information:

7 percent	38 percent	55 percent
verbal	cadence	nonverbal

It makes sense, then, to pay attention to visual or nonverbal cues in delivering important messages about behavior.

Our culture provides us with a vocabulary of gestures that students will understand with little explanation:

Zip across your lips	*Be quiet*
Finger across your throat	*You could be in big trouble*
Slowly shake your head	*No, no, no!*

Two fingers pointed at your eyes, then at student	*I'm watching you*
Raise eyebrows, disgusted look	*Are you kidding?*

Then, of course, there's your Business Face:

An enhancement of the Business Face is the Laser Stare—also known as the Look or the Hairy Eyeball, useful for gaining compliance from the group or from individuals. When using the Laser Stare, there's no need to speak until you have compliance. Then compliment.

If one student is inattentive or engaged in unacceptable behavior, you might use a low voice with your Laser Stare. Give one request at a time and wait for compliance.

Advanced Body Language

Building on the Laser Stare, you can create a Pregnant Pause. Stand in front of your class, wearing your Business Face and the Laser Stare. Don't say a word. Clear your throat if necessary. The silence should be deafening as the class quickly settles down without your speaking or wasting valuable energy. Always compliment compliance: "You are a terrific class."

If they don't get it, explain. Have them practice their response until it becomes an established routine.

Components of the Pregnant Pause

Business Face

Laser Stare

Wait for *total* compliance

Clear throat, as needed

"Excuse me?" if needed

A final enhancement is the Royal Move. This is designed to work with individual perpetrators.

Components of the Royal Move

Turn around and point both feet at the "perp"

Move in

Softly say his name and stay close to him

Laser Stare

Let your body do the talking

Lean in and prompt him back to work

If you decide to use sound effects with the Royal Move—that is, give a verbal command—always wait five to ten seconds before repeating it. Kids need time to process the direction and comply.

Visual Aids

Traffic control makes extensive and effective use of signals—from red lights to stop signs and one-way arrows. You can adapt this strategy for your classroom. This example makes use of a parrot, but you could use any animal—perhaps the class mascot.

Hang your movement control indicator in a prominent place in the classroom, and use the dial to give directions.

Free movement
Permission only
NO movement

The same little fellow, or his twin, can be used for Noise Control.

Silence
Whisper level
Table voices

A simple definition for *good* noise or movement and *bad* noise or movement is this:

> *If your movement or noise infringes on the rights of others, it is bad noise or movement. If the class is working in a group, I should hear students busily talking and not be able to identify any one voice . . . good noise. If I hear your voice over the other voices, it is bad noise.*

Voice Control

You'll recall that a couple of pages back, we learned that next to nonverbal language, students tended to learn from something called *cadence*. This means: it's not what you say, it's how you say it. You can use your voice as a valuable teaching tool.

Normal voice	Instructional mode
Lower voice	Focusing attention
Whisper	Command alertness
Loud voice	I mean business

Develop a Business Voice to go with your Business Face. Enunciate and speak slowly to underscore the seriousness of your concerns. And use this technique sparingly.

As effective as they are, nonverbal strategies and voice control will not resolve all the behavioral issues you may face in your classroom. Sometimes you need to talk one-on-one with particular students to work out difficulties in their behavior.

The One-Minute Correction

Enforce rules with an immediate reprimand.

Tell the student what he or she did wrong.

Explain how you feel.

Pause, let it sink in.

The Private Appeal

Use your hand or finger to direct the student to an area just outside the classroom.

While you're standing in the doorway, tell the class to resume their work.

Outside, you can invite cooperation or give a reprimand, as needed.

After a corrective lecture, it may be useful to have the child repeat the main points of the discussion so you know he or she understands your message.

See Me After Class

"See me after class." These words allow you to let a student know he or she has a problem without taking time away from the class activity. To interrupt the class even less, write "See me after class" on a card or note. You simply place the card on the student's desk—no words are exchanged. Or perhaps you'll need to provide a warning, if the student tries to talk: "Not now!"

See me before lunch.
We need a heart-to-heart talk.

I'd love to tell you you're a great kid.
Let's share your good work at home.

Some teachers use "see me" cards for both positive reinforcement and reprimand. For some students, the "see me" card will mean trouble; for others, it will mean a reward for sustained effort, consideration, good citizenship, or academic progress.

Staying the Course

Sometimes when a child is asked to stop an unacceptable behavior, his or her first instinct will be to "up the stakes"—in other words, keep on doing the same thing, just louder or faster. In a soft voice, calmly redirect the student until you get compliance.

When a student is creating a problem, approach the student and do one or all of the following, whatever it takes:

- Take a couple of relaxed breaths.
- Use a Laser Stare.
- Hang out in the area until the problem is over.
- Prompt the student by tapping on his or her desk.

The deep breaths are for you, ensuring you remain calm. In *The Godfather, Part 2*, Michael Corleone unemotionally kisses his brother (who has betrayed

the family) "goodbye—" before the brother gets the ultimate punishment. The lesson here is to calmly (calm is control) say, "You did the crime, now you have to do the time. Let's talk about an appropriate consequence."

Over the course of the school year, you may find that your class nibbles away at your management system. From time to time, you'll need to reassert your rules, procedures, and standards of behavior. If you feel this is happening, get a good night's sleep. Then go back to school and let your class know who is in charge. Take back control of your classroom.

Put on your Business Face.

Remember, you are the alpha dog!

Review the rules and consequences.

Deal quickly with perpetrators.

Take no prisoners.

Criticism, like rain, should be gentle enough to nourish a man's growth without destroying his roots.
    —Frank A. Clark (quoted in Reader's Digest
    Association, 1997)

Being in charge of your classroom and maintaining a good learning environment can be done, for the most part, with firmness and consistency—and a recognition that you love your young learners and want the very best for all of them.

Chapter 7

Handling Difficult Situations

IN SPITE OF MY BEST EFFORTS to establish a classroom structure and encourage good discipline, I occasionally face a challenge to my classroom management strategy. It's my job to ensure that my students never suffer—emotionally and physically, or simply from a loss of instructional time—as a result of the bad behavior of their peers.

I believe that most students will never cause trouble, and only a few pose any serious or continuous problem. Students who are overactive or intrusive in my classroom's operation can disturb my academic program without intending any harm. I do my best to find positive ways of defusing these issues.

I'm always ready when necessary to step into the middle and bring any conflict to a quick and peaceful end. I also have formal strategies for making sure difficult students are informed of their situation and that appropriate corrective action is taken.

Through all this, I recognize the need to manage my own emotions. When people lose their cool, they get a twenty-minute burst of adrenalin. I think of the damage that can be done in twenty minutes, and I do my best to divert any negative energy I feel.

In this chapter, I'll describe some strategies for handling the most serious discipline issues.

Overactive Kids and Clowns

Most of the youngsters who create classroom disturbances aren't "bad"—they just have more energy, a greater need for attention, and less self-control than their peers. Some simple strategies will help control the overactive kids.

Many a little Arnoldo suffers from "multi-quasi-neurological deficits": ants in their pants. Consider appointing your Arnoldo to the prestigious position of class gofer. Keep him busy with clerical duties—getting mail, helping keep attendance, doing housekeeping chores, making deliveries—any creative delegation that occurs to you. Keep him so busy he hardly ever gets in trouble any more.

Another strategy for overactive students involves setting limitations. Assign an overactive student two desks. Place a line of masking tape on the floor between the desks. The student can move around as long as he is sitting at a desk or standing on the line.

Keep in mind that all kids need to move throughout the day—and so do you. Get a tape or CD from a record store—*Hot! Hot! Hot! Dance Songs* is one—and when you see that the kids are getting fidgety, put on the music and let them sing and dance for a few minutes.

The Personal Gofer strategy, which works with overactive youngsters, can be adapted for use with the class clown. If you let the active child move around, also let the little entertainer perform—but on your schedule.

The Arnoldo Bianco Show
starring
Arnoldo Bianco

Make a deal with this little Arnoldo that if there are no disruptions during a specified period, he will have five minutes to perform at the end of the day.

Pest Control

Some students will seek your attention not with jokes but with questions in an endless stream. If you don't manage their interruptions, you'll lose time for instructional work, and you're bound to find yourself getting irritated with this little pest.

Set up an "interruption economy" with this kid. Give him a number of chips at the beginning of each day, and tell him he's got to buy your time with a chip.

Carrying a Large Toolbox

In this chapter and the last two, you've seen a great variety of techniques for managing your classroom, from building a positive, trouble-resistant environment to dealing with relatively minor miscreants.

Good teachers have a large toolbox and a variety of tools. If the only tool you have is a hammer—I'm the boss and you will obey me—you'll treat everyone like a nail. Keep in mind that

The same boiling water that softens the carrots hardens the eggs.

Good teachers know how to choose the right tool for the situation—something that will accomplish the goal with the least effort.

This can be as simple as a cardboard trifold. The trifold turns student desks into private study corrals. Putting up a student's trifold will isolate someone who is distracted by—or distracting from—the rest of the class. The trifolds also provide a little privacy for tests or silent reading.

Celebrating Small Victories

It's important to remain optimistic in dealing with behavioral problems. Instead of waiting to win the war before you celebrate, watch for all the little victories en route.

Baby steps are common with behavioral problems.

Keep brief, anecdotal, *dated* records.

Monitor progress over a period of weeks.

Celebrate or seek new interventions.

Keep in mind that your students aren't the only ones making progress. Each episode is recorded in your "internal teacher," so more episodes mean more knowledge, an increase in your ability to respond "automatically" to new students and new situations.

Dealing with Hostility

A not uncommon behavior problem is hostility—kids who have a problem with anger control or maybe are just having a bad day. You'll need to subdue the outbreak before it spreads.

- Get the person to a private area—perhaps outside the classroom.
- Take notes, if possible.
- Listen to the problem, and validate the student's feelings.
- Ask: What would you like me to do?
- Discuss options and alternatives.
- Document the outcome.
- Make and *keep* commitments.

Sometimes the hostilities may involve two students. After talking with the antagonists, you may want to keep them apart for a while, or for the whole term.

Inevitably, you will from time to time experience a problem that's so challenging or so intense and immediate that the usual strategies don't fit. Some of these actions, which should invoke the "severe" clause of your consequences system, include physical harm to another student, profanity, and insubordination.

Your immediate response should be

Desist Commands

Stop!

Absolutely *not!*

No way!

Help is coming.

The Broken Record

When a student is very upset and you're concerned that physical harm may occur, repeat a directed command again and again, until calm is restored.

I know you're upset, but you can't hurt anyone.

I feel your frustration, but you can't hurt him.

Your anger may be justified, but you can't harm her.

It sounds like you got a bad deal, but no person is allowed to hurt a classmate.

Averting Violence

If your class includes a bully, you may find yourself dealing with potential violence or intimidation more frequently. There are a variety of approaches you might try.

- Talk to the bully and describe the situation as you see it.
- Use humor to work your way out of the problem.
- Refuse to give in.
- Ignore the bully.
- Walk away.
- Avoid "problem" kids.

Some actions are always a good idea when confronted with a bully:

- Do not fight.

- Tell someone in charge.

- Use your brain to find a creative solution.

- Think of yourself as a strong person.

Violence may also turn up in the form of a spontaneous fight between two students. It's your job to break it up. Here's how.

- Get help.

- Dismiss the audience.

- Identify yourself as in charge.

- Concentrate on the aggressor.

- Remove the nonagressor.

- Make a report.

Discipline Tickets

Once the immediate crisis is over—or in situations in which consistent bad behavior doesn't involve a crisis—you can use a system of tickets to make sure the offender understands the seriousness of the situation. The ticket also makes a permanent record of the episode.

The first level of discipline tickets remains in the classroom. You will establish the format of the ticket, but it is filled out by the offending student or students. On the form, the student writes

- What happened

- Why I believe it happened

- What my part was

- What alternative behavior I could have used

- What I will do next time

The classroom ticket should also include a place for comments from the teacher, monitor, or other adult who witnessed the event. It should be signed by student, teacher, and parents.

Finally, the classroom ticket has a list of consequences in increasing severity, along with a checkmark next to the consequence for this incident.

Another Notch

As a last resort, some kids end up being sent to the principal's office. Teachers should work with the principal to develop a ticket that's used in these cases. It needs to be carefully thought out, as the ticket is excellent documentation for use at parent conferences or in a possible referral.

At the very least the ticket should contain

- The reason the student is being sent

- The teacher's recommendation for action

- A communication from the principal's office to the teacher on what will be done—it returns to the classroom with the student

- The signatures of everyone involved

So far, we've talked mostly about managing your classroom and the behavior of your students. But in some of the situations you confront, you will also need to manage your own emotions. In a touchy discipline situation, or in dealing with conflict and hostility, some teachers overreact. Fearing that they might lose control, they amplify the situation.

Crisis Management

As you confront a crisis, keep this list of Do's and Don'ts close to your heart.

Do

Remain calm

Use a respectful tone of voice

Watch your body language

Take all threats seriously

Assist with problem solving and resolution

Don't

Panic or overreact

Ignore the situation

Get into a power struggle

Threaten anyone

Give in to emotional outbursts

Of course, in some situations, you need to act immediately. In other cases, however, a little time won't change anything—except perhaps your ability to deal appropriately with the situation. People tend to make worse decisions when they are *Hungry, Angry, Lonely,* and *Tired* (HALT). Watch your actions when you are in one of the HALT areas. Consider whether you can invoke

The 24-Hour Rule

When you find yourself about to "lose it," tell your adversary:

I'm pretty upset right now, and I would like to put this on hold and meet with you first thing in the morning.

We are both having a difficult time with this, so I promise to call you tomorrow to review our options.

The bridge between hope and despair is a good night's sleep. A little rest can make the difference between this . . .

. . . and this

Have a heart that never hardens, and a temper that never fires,
and a touch that never hurts.
—Charles Dickens (quoted in Reader's Digest Association,
1997)

There may be days when the normal barrage of problems might have a tendency to harden any heart. You must remember that classroom life is a package deal. The disagreeable predicaments and negative experiences are far outweighed by the many positive and extraordinary happenings— and the opportunity to enrich the young lives entrusted to your care.

AS A TEACHER, I'm a classroom manager, making about five hundred decisions every day. No wonder I'm tired! To conserve my energy and reduce my stress level, I delegate as many tasks as possible, and I enlist other adults in a team effort to educate our kids.

My nearest and dearest allies are the students in my classroom. Many classroom tasks can be done by kids, if I take the time to carefully instruct them, demonstrate the process, and model the finished product. I take care to praise their efforts. While they're helping me, they learn valuable skills, and they enjoy the opportunity to be my helpers.

Classroom aides and other teachers are also available to provide assistance. Sometimes I also use older students or adult volunteers to do tasks that might put a strain on my time.

Of course, my very best allies are the parents of my students. They already have an interest in the student's educational outcome, so they come to me motivated. It's up to me to show them how we can work together most effectively.

In this chapter, I illustrate some ways to enlist others in achieving your goals.

Your Study Buddy

One of your students is out sick. Someone will need to get that student up-to-date on what's been done in class and what assignments might have been missed. Of course, you could do this, but it's an easy job to delegate.

Early in the school year, pair off your kids into "study buddies" and assign them a range of tasks they can do for each other.

The biggest duty for study buddies is to put together a class aid box—(you provide the box) with all the tests, papers, newsletters, and other items the student has missed. When the student returns, a box filled with makeup work is ready and waiting.

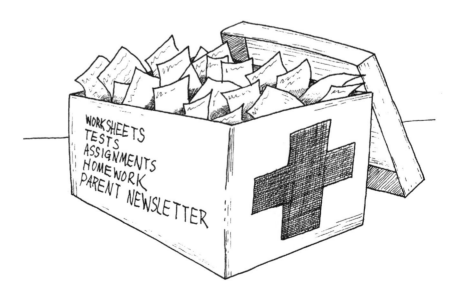

But study buddies can be useful throughout the year. You might set up a "3 Before Me" system in your classroom to cut down on the number of questions you have to answer each day.

- Ask your study buddy.
- Check around the classroom for a chart, worksheet, schedule, or bulletin board with the answer you need.
- Ask another student.

Students are also watching each other. They're competitive and they're empathetic. You can take advantage of this by using the Ripple Effect.

The Ripple Effect

You Say . . .	Students . . .
I can see that several people have already completed the assignment.	Work faster—no one wants to be last.
Table 4 people are correct. Group 2, very responsible work!	Follow the model. Everyone wants praise and approval.
I can always count on you to know what to do next.	Feel proud of their accomplishment.
Use Laser Stare and command on one student.	Make sure they're complying—no one wants to get in trouble.

Class Meetings

If you consider your students as citizens of your classroom, each of them has an interest in helping to keep the peace so that positive education can go forward. When a situation arises that affects the classroom environment, consider holding a class meeting.

You might want to schedule regular class meetings to deal with any problem submitted by you or a student. Here are some guidelines:

Direct the discussion toward solving the problem.

Keep the atmosphere nonjudgmental and nonpunitive—avoid fault finding.

The solutions should not include punishment.

You and your students should be seated in a tight circle.

Class meetings should be held often and never exceed thirty to forty-five minutes, depending on the age of students.

Class meetings can be particularly effective in handling conflict if there's arguing or fighting going on among your students.

To use class meetings as a way to resolve conflict

- Set guidelines for the discussion
- Clarify what happened
- Explore different points of view—give every side a chance to speak
- Identify the cause of the conflict
- Develop agreement about the cause
- Develop agreement about how to resolve the conflict
- Specify an action plan
- Evaluate group efforts

Peer Confrontation

A variation on the class meeting is the peer confrontation strategy, a rather controversial new approach in which peers—perhaps the whole class—assist in the disciplinary process. It's controversial because it makes the misbehaving student the center of attention—which may have been his or her goal in the first place. However, if other strategies have failed, it's worth a try.

First, you stop the class and describe the inappropriate behavior. Then you ask a series of questions for class discussion.

Using a Buddy Teacher

Another last-ditch strategy with difficult students is to enlist the assistance of a buddy teacher. Before you engage this plan,

- Have a talk with the student, and warn him that consequences may follow his actions.

- Send the student to a time-out area of your classroom.

If neither works, make arrangements with a fellow teacher to send that student to another class. Sometimes it's effective to send the child to a classroom that's two or three grade levels above or below yours.

Your buddy teacher will need to know when a student is coming and how long his "respite" should be. In some cases, teachers have permanently swapped students—at the same grade level—with great success.

Enlisting Student or Adult Tutors

Some of your students would probably benefit from extra attention or tutoring. Your school may have a program for enlisting adult volunteers, and right within your school you may have older students (they should be a few years older) who would enjoy the opportunity to work with youngsters. Consider making these potential helpers part of your overall educational strategy.

Here are some guidelines for tutor programs:

- Give all tutors a training session.

- Have enough tutors so that no single person is overburdened.

- Match the best tutors with the neediest students.

- Provide a physical space where tutors and students can work.

- Provide a party or other reward for the tutors.

Substitute Teachers

All schools have a formal program for providing teachers with help—it's called substitute teachers. These folks are important allies, and it's to your benefit if they are well prepared.

You might want to make a videotape that the substitute teacher can play that gives your students important information and instruction.

Substitute teachers should get a folder that includes

Schedules and duties

Class rules and procedures

Where to find stuff

Attendance, lunch, and dismissal procedures

Information on fire drills and location of office

You'll also want to ask substitute teachers for feedback.

Were plans adequate?

How did students behave? [briefly]

How would they correct instructions?

Do they have other comments?

Your Very Own Mentor

When you first start teaching, it's a good idea to look around for an experienced teacher to be your mentor. You'll want someone you share attitudes and interests with and someone whose teaching style you admire. You might ask to spend time in your mentor's classroom, or in the classrooms of as many senior teachers as you can.

You probably have more than one *internal* mentor—a teacher you had in the past whose approach motivated you to complete an assignment. Maybe you had a teacher who inspired you to pursue a career in education. Think of the good experiences—and bad—you've had as a student, and let these help you frame your own teaching style.

Although this book provides the kind of advice a mentor teacher might offer, there's really no substitute for a living, breathing person who can celebrate your early victories and help you learn from your early mistakes.

And don't forget that one day, it will be your turn to play mentor.

Your Most Powerful Allies

Of course, parents are your most powerful partners in furthering the educational goals of your students. Next to the students themselves, they have the most at stake. You must let parents know what their responsibilities are.

"Little Arnoldo's success depends on

Making sure he's in school
Limiting his TV time
Having reading material in your home
Making sure he spends time reading

You can help me by making sure these things happen."

Building the Parent Partnership

Parents have a strong influence over a child's behavior in school. Research suggests that 85 percent of discipline problems in school are related to problems at home. To correct a student's behavioral problems, you need to connect with parents.

When a student is making trouble, you need to hold parents responsible by

- Sharing the specific behavior(s) that needs improvement

- Promoting a relationship that garners their positive support

- Having them commit to corrective actions *they* will take if behavior does not improve

At home, parents have primary responsibility for what their children do and don't do. Here are some suggestions to share with them.

It's a good idea to ask students to give you an hourly schedule of how they spend their afterschool time. At parent conferences, you can check these against what the parents observe. Your goal should be to raise parent awareness about how much time their children spend watching TV. The average student watches twenty-nine hours of television every week—far too much.

MORE

*reading alone
*reading with
  someone
*playing sports

LESS

*TV
*eating
*sleeping

A Place to Study

Stress to parents that students need a private place to do homework and study. This should be away from the living area where other family members might provide distractions. It should never include a television.

Parent-Teacher Conferences

Parent-teacher conferences are always eye-openers. After you meet some parents, you will have a better understanding of their kids. It's important to prepare for a conference carefully.

Plan and write outcome goals.

Prepare and review pupil information folder.

Use a professional setting.

Allow no interruptions.

It's always good to use the P word—partnership—as soon as possible in your conference. Some other good words to rely on begin with F: feel, felt, and found.

Here are some other conversational guidelines:

Ask the parents what they would like to achieve through the conference. Do they have any specific questions about your program? About their child's progress?

Don't bring your own life stories into the conversation.

Use your listening skills and focus on what the other person is saying.

Rephrase and reflect what the other person said to be sure you understood.

Jointly formulate an action plan.

Parent-Teacher Action Contract

Depending on a student's progress and needs, you may want to create a formal parent-teacher action contract. The contract should

- Identify areas of concern
- Establish a daily monitoring system between home and school, with all parties signing off
- Be easy to complete and understand
- Provide for adjustments as needed

A Model Contract

Arnoldo will:

Start and stop work promptly

Respond to requests with one reminder

Complete assignments

Interact with classmates in a positive way

Show respect for others

Staying in Touch

Any good relationship takes regular communication. Meeting once or twice a year at a parent conference or parents' night won't establish that kind of link between school and home.

Personal notes are a great way to connect with parents because they're directed at each individual student and his or her progress. Teaching supply catalogs provide note forms that let you send the original copy of your note to the parents and keep a copy in your individual student folder.

To: _____   Date_____

_____

_____

_____

_____

_____

_____

_____

_____

_____

_____

_____

_____

Teacher _____   Parent _____

You might also consider a newsletter (desktop publishing makes them easy to create and duplicate) to keep parents informed about activities involving the whole class.

The bell that rings a sermon calls not upon the preacher only,
but upon the congregation to come,
so this bell calls us all.

—John Donne (quoted in Shanahan, 1999)

This is another way of saying "It takes a village," I suppose. Although you are master of your classroom, you will be wise to enlist all the help you can get. When you reach out to others for help in achieving your educational mission, you not only take the pressure off yourself but also pay others the compliment of enlisting them as partners.

Chapter 9

Joining the Educational Team at Your School

AS A MASTER TEACHER, I advocate teamwork with my colleagues. I work hard at "bringing something to the party," and I understand that a positive group effort can yield a quality finished product. A great deal of research indicates that a school family that plays together is strong and vibrant. Work should be more fun than "fun." As "Confucius" said, "Choose a job you love, and you will never have to work a day in your life."

I contribute to this environment by bringing to my colleagues the same culture of appreciation I have built in my classroom. Everyone needs encouragement and support—my principal, school staff, and fellow teachers, as well as my students.

I also take my share of the planning and committee work that has to be done so that the school can grow and improve in its educational mission. I'm willing to work with others to achieve our mutual goals. My main focus is on having the best possible program for kids and my fellow professionals—whether this means creating change or relying on tradition.

In this chapter, I'll suggest some ways to become a valued member of your school's educational team.

Make Your Principal Look Good

The principal is the leader of your school team. Giving the principal your sincere support is a good way to help the school move forward and to make sure you'll have the principal's support if you ever need it. Here are some ways to get that done.

Find out one of your principal's frustrations or worries—it's easy to do, just listen—and help eliminate it.

Chances are that one of those frustrations has to do with budget. Do what you can to keep expenses in line.

Before you go to your principal with a problem, think of some possible solutions to suggest.

Keep your principal informed about what's happening in your classroom and in students' home environment if that's relevant.

Praise the principal when praise is warranted—no one is so important they don't need a kind word.

Take good care of your school's clients—your students and their parents.

Instead of Cursing the Darkness . . .

Every school has a combination of pickles and cucumbers in its employee salad. Some of the pickles may be old-timers, but a lot of veteran teachers remain cucumbers throughout their career. One way to tell a pickle is by the sour face.

Here are some other pickle alerts you might hear around school:

"I tried that years ago, and it didn't work."

"That's not the way it's done around here."

"Let me tell you about *her*."

"Not with this principal."

"Why do more than you need to?"

"Parents are always that way."

Pickles are also known as . . .

Cynics   people who smell flowers
and look for the grave, and

Pessimists   "I should have known
this would happen."

. . . Light a Candle

The surest way to survive as a cucumber is to hang out with other cucumbers. But if you still find yourself "in a pickle,"

What a Pickle!

- Tell the pickle, "I'm new here, and I don't know anything about that. Thanks for your opinion."

- Light candles in the teachers' lounge: *Don't contribute to the gossip.*

- Find a mentor among the more senior teachers and get advice on how to handle any troublesome gossip.

- Don't play the blame game that goes on in many schools. If there's a problem, light candles instead of cursing the darkness. Seek solutions, not people to blame.

> *If Columbus had an advisory committee, he would probably still be at the dock.*
> —former Supreme Court Justice Arthur Goldberg

There is some wisdom in what Justice Goldberg has to say, but committees are still one of the best ways to

- Make progress
- Use the collective brainpower of many people
- Foster a culture of empowerment

Join a Committee . . .

Particularly when change is required or new programs have to be developed, assigning a committee to help make plans means you get more good ideas. Also, the people who have to live with the decision help make it—if they take ownership of the project, resistance is less likely.

I'm involved, and therefore I'm committed to this project.

Sometimes in a committee a leader will may emerge who can energize the troops and lead the charge. Or the committee will form a bond that helps move a project forward.

. . . And Help Make It Work

Chances are, your career as a teacher will include service on more than one or two committees. A good start is the best way to ensure a good outcome, so it's useful to make sure everyone's clear about these issues:

- How often will we meet and for how long?

- What outcome do we want?

- When are we expected to complete this project?

- What is each person's responsibility?

- Are there any potential problems or concerns that we should know about?

Some other practical strategies can help move things along:

- Divide the job into components and make a timetable for completing each.

- Keep notes on progress and hurdles so it's easier next time.

- Make a few simple rules to cover how you'll operate. For example, ensure that everyone gets to make his or her case, not just the most vocal members.

Help Plan Events

Many school committees are assigned to plan particular events or programs. Because these tend to happen year after year, it's helpful to keep an eye on the long-term outlook when you're doing the immediate planning.

- At your first meeting review overall goals and pass out assignments to individuals.
- Generate a report as you go along that makes a record of what worked and what didn't, so you can work out the bugs.
- Celebrate the planning group's accomplishments and reward participants.
- Make sure to credit the movers and shakers in writing.
- After the event, assign responsibilities for next year, so people can be preparing year-round.
- Don't just rely on veterans. Relatively inexperienced, creative people can bring new eyes and new energy to a project.

Other committees will be assigned to respond to particular school problems or to review new educational mandates to see how they can be implemented in your school. This means

Change!

Adapt to Change

Change almost always produces reaction, resistance, and rejection. You can make it go more easily.

- Phase changes in over an extended period, so people can adjust gradually.
- Listen and learn from the loyal opposition—and respond to their good ideas.
- Recruit and convert support people.
- Vary your approach to the change—one explanation or rationale may not fit all.

Another C word that shows up frequently at school is

Conflict!

The win-lose mentality seems to be so much a part of the American psyche that it's difficult to change. Getting your school team to use a win-win strategy for accomplishing goals will take time and patience.

Manage Conflict

In fact, the best way is usually "the third way": respecting everyone's contributions and accomplishments.

- Refocus the spotlight from right versus wrong to what can be done to address the challenges.
- Provide supporting logic and data.
- Study the opposition's concerns and see whether their perceptions can be incorporated in a new solution.
- Ask: What's in the best interest of our students?
- Go back to the drawing board and redraw the plan.

You may be wondering why I haven't introduced another C word here:

Compromise!

Everybody thinks very highly of compromise, but the fact is that compromise is usually an attempt to satisfy all the participants rather than maximize the outcome. So I say:

Don't compromise—optimize!

Optimizing is collective thought that goes beyond reconciliation to a place where all participants feel they got more than half a loaf, and everyone likes the finished product. How to do it?

- Create a critical mass of "we's" who are on the same page striving to attain the goals.

- Educate and communicate until the number of "they's" diminishes.

- Adapt your approach if it will convert more "they's."

- Involve the "they's" in decision making.

- Combine diverse positions and interests in a win-win position.

Sometimes it is best not to make a decision until there is consensus.

Lose Gracefully

There comes a time in every teacher's life when you've just got to suck it in and admit that you lost this time. Maybe you were wrong—if that's it, then you ought to publicly fess up and pledge to support the new direction.

Before you let your emotions show, look outside and make sure you parked your ego at the door. Remember, this is about the mission and goals of the school community and the welfare of your students. It's not about you.

If you feel you must criticize the decision, make sure you stick to the idea and not the people who promoted it. A personal affront to any member of the community creates a climate of dissension and distrust. A wound never heals smooth—there's always a scar.

If you've reached a bridge, however, and you've got a torch in your hand, think twice before setting the fire. Speaking too candidly about your response to a perceived injustice may just make things worse.

If you must speak, state your position or indignation in the most controlled and objective terms possible. Then leave with decorum and dignity. Burning bridges is rarely a good career move for any long-term teacher. If your only option is to move on, "go gracefully into the night."

Join Your School's Educational Team

But let's assume you never see a bridge you want to burn. You enjoy your teaching, and you like the people with whom you work. You've made it—you're part of the educational team at your school. Here's how to recognize a successful team:

The worth and dignity of all team members are recognized.

Everyone knows the team's mission and understands what his or her decision-making role is within the team.

Everyone pursues the team's goals—and only those goals.

Rank distinctions are minimized. The focus is on group goals and achievements.

All team members value and practice good listening skills.

The team celebrates victories and gives personal recognition when it's deserved.

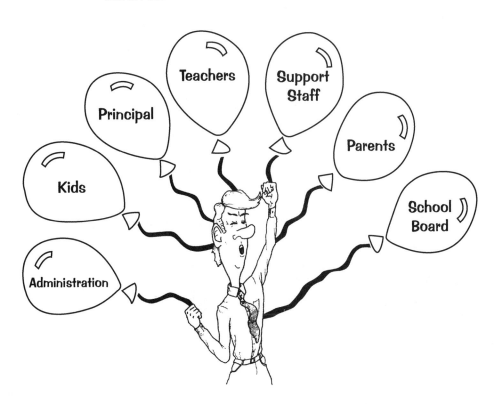

Build Team Spirit

Within your school, build team spirit with social acknowledgments.

Establish a school social committee to plan social activities throughout the year.

Schedule parties for a Five-Year-Plus or Ten-Year-Plus Club to honor the service of long-term employees.

Hold an annual awards lunch to honor teachers and support staff.

Schedule an assembly at the end of each month to honor students.

Most of all, look forward and encourage creativity. Make your school not just a culture of appreciation but also a culture of risk takers, where people are encouraged to think of ways they can make things better.

> *One room, one team, one coffee pot, one vision.*
> —Mike Vance (quoted in Capodagli and Jackson, 1999)

A school without dreams is like a day without sunshine. What are your school's dreams?

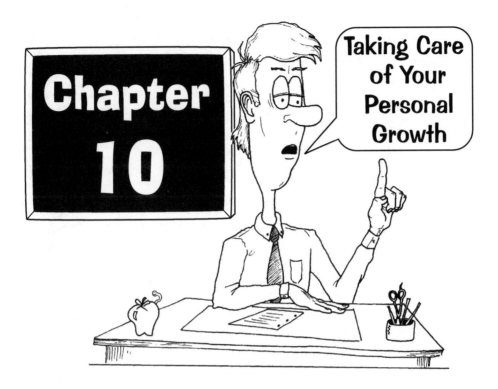

IN THE UNITED STATES, one in four teachers leaves the profession within five years. To be one of the survivors—to become a master teacher—I need to take care of myself personally and professionally. I realize that I need to continually increase my body of knowledge and to hone my professional skills.

I also need to keep my perspective. My family and friends are the most important things in my life, and I make sure to set aside enough time and energy to take care of their needs and to enjoy their company. Next in line are my students. My teaching is my lifelong love, and I make decisions that are student centered. Sometimes it is hard to balance personal needs and professional demands, but I do my best.

I am attuned to messages from my conscience, and I behave accordingly. I understand that life offers temptations of all types and varieties, and I build strength, integrity, and character to help me avoid these pitfalls. As much as humanly possible, I learn from yesterday's mistakes, bury them, and prepare for today and tomorrow.

In this chapter, I discuss some strategies you can use to survive the difficulties inherent in education and to become a master teacher.

Professional Development

Athletes are always in training. Doctors go back to school from time to time to learn new techniques. Teachers need to find ways to stay in top condition, too.

- Visit another classroom or another school to see how other teachers do their work.

- Attend a workshop or conference related to educational skills or your content area.

- Take a professional or personal development class.

- Set up a small group where teachers at the same grade level or in the same content area can share experiences and information.

- Read, read, read, read, read. And then read.

You might create a professional library of books and periodicals to share with colleagues, or look at new periodicals regularly and copy journal articles that are pertinent to you and your colleagues. Share them.

Of course, you'll want to support your school library collection. You can encourage parents to raise money to enhance the school's library, and invite local businesses to become school partners and contribute to your school's reading and other information resources.

Why not establish a classroom library that everyone can contribute to and draw from?

Getting Legal Help

Sometimes teachers will find themselves in need of legal help. This may be the result of your own actions or of your school's policies or performance. Either way, going it alone is not an option.

- Forget the lawyer jokes. If someone threatens legal action—and, in particular, if you have to go to court—you need to have a lawyer. Local, state, and national bar associations are excellent sources.

- If the legal action is connected to the school district or school board, their lawyer may *not* be representing you. Make sure you have personal legal representation if you need it.

- Keep in close communication with your principal on all legal matters; if it's allowed, stay in touch with the district's or school board's lawyer as well.

- Document all your contacts related to the lawsuit, and provide copies to school and district officials as required.

Dealing with the Media

Suppose a reporter calls and wants to talk to you about a story. Be flattered for about two seconds. Then be careful. Be very careful. Being misquoted or quoted out of context is not a rare occurrence. Understand that this can happen to you.

- It's difficult if not impossible to unring the bell. The printed word—accurate or inaccurate—has a tremendous impact on readers, and no correction can ever undo all the damage.

- If you don't think well on your feet, if you're not an expert on the subject or event of interest, or if you simply would prefer not to do a personal interview, *just say no.* The best response is to refer reporters to your supervisor. Don't explain. According to the journalist's rulebook, anything you say to a reporter once you've been introduced can turn up on tomorrow's front page.

- If you've agreed to an interview and you or the school is at fault, don't try to cover it up. State the facts, apologize if appropriate, and make a commitment to future improvement. Make sure what you say conforms to the school's official position.

- Press releases should be carefully worded and concise, containing accurate and objective information and the name and phone number and e-mail address of a person whom reporters can contact. Have a couple of people proofread the release, and make sure the final version is approved by your boss.

- Not the *New York Times* but some news outlets will actually let you review what they write before it's printed; others will give you a copy of any direct quotes they plan to use before publication. It never hurts to ask.

- If a reporter makes a mistake, demand a correction.

Avoiding Burnout

You're a committed teacher.   You're burned out.

There isn't a great deal of space between those two situations. If you're devoted to your profession and your school, it's easy to be lulled into concentrating too much of your energy on the job at the expense of other important aspects of life.

Whether or not you're married and have children—but especially if that is true—you "have a life" outside of school that needs your energy. Ignoring the overall quality of your life—including your physical, mental, and moral well-being—may have negative results not only for you and your family but also for your students and your teaching career.

Here are some surefire flame retardants for burnout:

- Exercise regularly

- Eat a nutritionally sound diet

- Spend time with family and friends

- Bring new ideas to the classroom

- Have fun—at home and in school

Take a Vacation

The best deterrent to burnout is some time off. A vacation, short or long, expensive or not. Traveling or staying home. Enjoying the great outdoors or the culture and excitement of a big city. Think about what type of vacation would be most restful and rejuvenating for you—and take it.

- Plan your vacation several months in advance, and watch the time in between disappear—your stress will go down while your morale goes up, just thinking about the warm, happy light at the end of the tunnel.

- Short getaways, even long weekends, can help you maintain a healthy balance of work and play. Place these respites strategically throughout the school year, and you'll reap long-term dividends that sustain you along the way.

- When you're thinking about the cost of a vacation, consider the cost of *not taking one.* The kinds of stress that vacations prevent can create mental and physical problems that are very expensive to fix.

- In between, make sure to schedule a weekly date night or night out. If your friends are also colleagues, limit shop talk to a short period of time or ban it altogether. Private time together builds lasting relationships, and lasting relationships are another deterrent to burnout.

Conscience is the inner voice that warns us somebody may be looking.

> —Henry Louis Mencken (quoted in Shanahan, 1999)

This quotation has a slightly cynical edge, unless you understand that the "somebody" who may be looking is your best self, the one you hope everyone sees.

Staying on the Side of the Angels

We all hear the distinctive, clear voice of conscience from time to time. Trouble is, we often ignore it.

If you lie in bed feeling troubled by a past action or a pending decision—or by something you didn't do—your unrest represents a clear warning that something isn't right. The only way to get rid of the anxiety you're feeling is to listen to your conscience again and this time follow its advice.

All men are tempted. There's no man that lives that can't be broken down, provided it is the right temptation, put in the right spot.

> —Henry Ward Beecher (quoted in Shanahan, 1999)

Avoid Temptation

Everyone faces temptation, most of us time and again. Acting on that temptation is what leads us to impending disaster. You can avoid crossing that line.

- Build a solid hedge around the dangerous ground of sex, money, power, false pride, control, and duplicity. *Do not cross it.*

- Talk to someone you trust about your temptation—your spouse, a trusted friend, a religious adviser, a professional counselor—and ask for his or her help: advice, a slap on the head, whatever it takes to keep you on the right side of the hedge.

- In that instant of weakness, remember that you have an independent will. You don't have to cave in.

- Beware the "shiny lures." Temptation is an expert fisherman who uses the most attractive bait to catch the prize.

- Just say no to

   Any "political deal" that is morally or ethically wrong

   The job of personally handling school funds; delegate

   Time-wasting activities that are not in the best interest of the kids

   The temptation to tell a lie

Take Positive Action

Doing nothing wrong isn't enough. Sometimes, *not* doing something is wrong. Let me share some sins of omission:

- Failing to attend seminars, workshops, and staff development experiences
- Not tending to the needs of your kids regardless of such variables as home background, nutrition, socioeconomic status, attitude, and motivation
- Allowing anyone to curse the darkness without demanding that he or she light a candle (approaching frustrations in a positive way can improve the school environment)
- Not encouraging the pursuit of new ventures and challenges

False Pride Versus Strong Ego

We all need a good healthy sense of confidence in our own abilities and a positive sense of our social worth. There's a big difference, however, between a big ego and a strong ego, between false pride and self-respect. False pride will eventually catch you by the tail and bring you down:

- Never forget what you were like when you were starting out, and treat everyone with the same respect you wanted to be shown back then.
- If you find yourself thinking you're "hot stuff," spend a day as a kindergarten teacher.
- Look in the mirror each day and praise the education gods for allowing you to contribute to the academic, social, and emotional growth of young learners.

A strong ego, on the other hand, helps you

- Accept praise gracefully and without fanfare, acknowledging the contributions of your team
- Be an active team player who celebrates the group's achievements
- Keep the spotlight on the group's objectives rather than your personal agenda
- Focus on the school's goal: making good things happen for kids

We all like to be liked. For teachers, though, it's important to keep an eye on the long-term goal while enjoying day-to-day popularity.

Popularity Versus Glory

You can be popular if you

- Remember the names of present and former students and their parents

- Have a pleasing, optimistic personality

- Display your wit and fabulous sense of humor

- Have a winning year or season

Long-term glory for a teacher is harder to achieve. It means

- Making a permanent contribution to kids' lives by establishing a program that benefits them for years to come

- Being there for your fellow teachers in a crisis

- Having a reputation for excellent rapport and cooperation with teachers and support staff

- Contributing something tangible to your classroom or school that will be an asset and source of pride for years to come

Building Character

Like professional growth, character building is a lifelong endeavor. Here are some of the materials:

- Let setbacks and mistakes roll into the past, and remain focused on the challenges and opportunities in your future.

- Give credit to everyone who supports you.

- Use self-talk not just to critique your performance but to give yourself personal accolades for a job well done.

- At the end of the day, give yourself praise points for positive achievements.

- Tell others when you think they've done a great job—celebrate their victories, not just your own.

- Listen to and learn from everyone you meet, including your young students.

- Never stop learning.

Conformity may be the curse of American education. From Bangor, Maine, to Tampa, Florida, from Tucson, Arizona, to Spokane, Washington, classrooms seem to be run much the same way. Either we have found the ultimate educational answer, or we're mired in a quagmire of sameness.

Being a conformist may be safe, especially if you're a teacher in a state without tenure, but it doesn't always lead to great teaching. Master teachers have a different outlook:

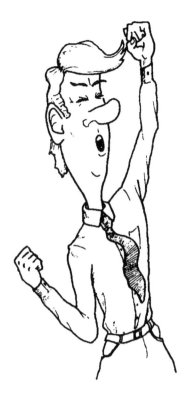

I am an experienced teacher, and I know who I am and what principles I espouse.

I live my mission: it is part of who I am and what I do.

My philosophy is so clear that my students and their parents can clearly articulate it.

I am an alpha educator; creative, diplomatic nonconformity is a way of life.

My motto: New ideas for a better tomorrow.

The biggest mistake you can make is to
believe you are working for someone else.
—"Bits and Pieces" (Reader's Digest Association, 1997)

People don't remember school districts or boards of education. They'll remember their school, of course, but it's their teachers who they will think of and tell stories about as they grow older. When great people are asked about who influenced their growth, they name teachers, not schools.

Your legacy is being created every day. Construct it with diligence and a passion for improving your teaching performance.

Run your classroom as though you owned it. When you make decisions, the standard should be: this is what I'd do if I owned this classroom.

Work hard, with dedication to your profession and your kids. This will pay dividends in accumulated knowledge throughout your career. Others will witness your devotion to being the very best teacher, and this reputation will serve you well.

Your amassed knowledge and experience will make you a future asset to any school that is fortunate enough to employ you.

Bibliography

Anderson, P. *Great Quotes from Great Leaders.* Franklin Lakes, N.J.: Career Press, 1997.

Bloom, B. S. "Time and Learning." *American Psychologist,* 1974, *29,* 682–688.

Breeden, T., and Eagan, E. *Positive Classroom Management.* Nashville, Tenn.: Incentive, 1997.

Canter, L., and Canter, M. *Assertive Discipline: A Take Charge Approach for Today's Educator.* Los Angeles: Canter and Associates, 1976.

Capodagli, B., and Jackson, L. *The Disney Way.* New York: McGraw Hill, 1999.

Charles, C. M. *Building Classroom Discipline.* New York: Longman, 1989.

Chernow, C., and Chernow, F. B. *Classroom Discipline Survival Guide.* West Nyack, N.Y.: Center for Applied Research in Education, 1989.

Cooper, J. M. *Classroom Teaching Skills.* Boston: Houghton Mifflin, 1999.

Covey, S. R. *The 7 Habits of Highly Effective People.* New York: Simon & Schuster, 1989.

Covey, S. R. *The 8th Habit.* New York: Free Press, 2004.

Cummings, C. *Winning Strategies for Classroom Management.* Alexandria, Va.: Association for Supervision and Curriculum Development, 2000.

Curwin, R. *The Fourth R.* Eau Claire, Wis.: Otter Creek Institute, 1999.

Curwin, R. L., and Mendler, A. N. *Discipline with Dignity.* Alexandria, Va.: Association for Supervision and Curriculum Development, 1988.

Dreikurs, R., Grunwald, B. B., and Pepper, F. C. *Maintaining Sanity in the Classroom.* New York: HarperCollins, 1971.

Ehrlich, E. *Amo, Amas, Amat and More.* New York: HarperCollins, 1985.

Evertson, C. M., and others. *Classroom Management for Elementary Teachers.* Needham Heights, Mass.: Allyn & Bacon, 1989.

Gardner, J. W. *On Leadership.* New York: Simon & Schuster, 1990.

Glasser, W. *Control Theory in the Classroom.* New York: Perennial Library, 1985.

Goldberg, M. "Portrait of Madeline Hunter." *Educational Leadership,* 1990, 47(5), 41–43.

Hunter, M., *Mastery Teaching.* El Segundo, Calif.: TIP Publications, 1982.

Jones, F. *Tools for Teaching.* Santa Cruz, Calif.: Fredrick H. Jones & Associates, 2000.

Kounin, J. *Discipline and Group Management in Classrooms.* Austin, Tex.: Holt, Reinhart and Winston, 1970.

Lipscomb, E. J., Webb, F. E., and Conn, P. (eds.). *The Several Worlds of Pearl S. Buck: Essays Presented at a Centennial Symposium, Randolph-Macon Woman's College, March 26-28, 1992.* Westport, Conn.: Greenwood Press, 1994.

Lombardi, V. *The Lombardi Rules.* New York:McGraw Hill, 2004.

MacKenzie, R. J. *Setting Limits in the Classroom.* Roseville, Calif.: Prima, 1996.

Maggio, R. *Quotations on Education.* Upper Saddle River, N.J.:Prentice Hall, 1997.

Mahle, B. *Power Teaching, Practical Tips for Teaching Adolescents.* Torrance, Calif.: Frank Schaffer, 1999.

Mauer, R. E. *Special Educator's Discipline Handbook.* West Nyack, N.Y.: Center for Applied Research in Education, 1988.

Palmer, P. *Change Magazine,* Nov.-Dec. 1997, 29(6), 14–21.

Partin, R. L. *Classroom Teacher's Survival Guide.* West Nyack, N.Y.: Center for Applied Research in Education, 1999.

Patton, G. S., Jr. *War as I Knew It.* Boston: Houghton Mifflin, 1995.

Peters, T. *The Pursuit of Wow.* New York: Vintage Books, 1994.

Reader's Digest Association. *Quotable Quotes.* Pleasantville, N.Y.: Reader's Digest Association, 1997.

Rhode, G., Jenson, W. R., and Reavis, H. K. *The Tough Kid Book.* Longmont, Colo.: Sopris West, 1992.

Ryan, K., and Cooper, J. *Those Who Can Teach.* Boston: Houghton Mifflin, 2000.

Shanahan, J. M. (ed.). *The Most Brilliant Thoughts of All Time (in Two Lines or Less).* New York: HarperCollins, 1999.

Sprick, R. S. *Discipline in the Secondary Classroom.* West Nyack, N.Y.: Center for Applied Research in Education, 1985.

Thompson, J. *Discipline Survival for Secondary Teacher.* Paramus, N.J.: Center for Applied Research in Education, 1998.

Timmons, J. *Entrepreneurial Mind: Winning Strategies for Starting, Renewing, and Harvesting.* Lawrence, Mass.: Brickhouse, 1989.

Watson, G. *Teacher Smart!* Paramus, N.J.: Center for Applied Research in Education, 1996.

Williamson, B. *Classroom Management: A Guidebook for Success.* Sacramento, Calif.: Dynamic Teaching Company, 1992.

Wong, H. *The First Days of School.* Sunnyvale, Calif.: Harry Wong, 1991.

Collected Quotes

Some people strengthen society just by the kind of people they are.
—John W. Gardner (1990)

Experience is the name everyone gives mistakes.
—Oscar Wilde (quoted in Shanahan, 1999)

Success is going from failure to failure without a loss of enthusiasm.
—Anonymous (quoted in Shanahan, 1999)

Tact is the knack of making a point without making an enemy.
—Sir Isaac Newton (quoted in Shanahan, 1999)

I will not let anyone walk through my mind with their dirty feet.
—Mahatma Gandhi (quoted in Shanahan, 1999)

If we had no faults of our own, we would not take so much pleasure in noticing those of others.
—Francois duc de la Rouchefoucauld
(quoted in Shanahan, 1999)

Integrity is not a conditional word. It does not blow in the wind or change with the weather. It is your inner image of yourself, and if you look in there and see a man who won't cheat, then you know he never will.

—John D. MacDonald (quoted in Reader's Digest Association, 1997)

Even if you're on the right track, you'll get run over if you just sit there.

—Will Rogers (quoted in Covey, 1989)

The quality of a person's life is in direct proportion to their commitment to excellence, regardless of their chosen field of endeavor.

—Vince Lombardi (2004)

We are what we repeatedly do. Excellence, then, is not an act, but a habit.

—Aristotle (quoted in Covey, 1989)

Yesterday is experience. Tomorrow is hope. Today is getting from one to the other the best we can.

—John M. Henry (quoted in Reader's Digest Association, 1997)

Children have never been good at listening to their elders, but they have never failed to imitate them.

—James Baldwin (quoted in Shanahan, 1999)

Nothing is particularly hard if you divide it into small jobs.

—Henry Ford (quoted in Anderson, 1997)

The more you prepare outside of class, the less you perspire in class. The less you perspire in class, the more you inspire in class.

—Ho Boon Tiong (quoted in Maggio, 1997)

There is no bigger sin than to do nothing when you could have done something.

—Unknown (quoted in Covey, 1989)

All the people like us are We, and everyone else is They.

—Rudyard Kipling (quoted in Shanahan, 1999)

Compromise makes a good umbrella but a poor roof.

—James R. Lowell (quoted in Reader's Digest Association, 1997)

Never tell people how to do things. Tell them what to do, and they will surprise you with their ingenuity.

—Tom Peters (1994)

We are more anxious to speak than to be heard.

—Henry David Thoreau (quoted in Shanahan, 1999)

Conscience is thoroughly well-bred and soon leaves off talking to those who do not wish to hear it.

—Samuel Butler (quoted in Shanahan, 1999)

The ant is knowing and wise; but he doesn't know enough to take a vacation.

—Clarence Day (quoted in Shanahan, 1999)